The Three Woes
A Guide to Understanding Revelation and End Time Prophecies

The Three Woes
A Guide To Understanding Revelation and End Time Prophecies

Copyright © 2020 by Barney Rapp - All rights reserved.
No part of this book may be reproduced in any form, except for brief excerpts in reviews or articles, without written permission from the publisher.

For permission, write:	Technisys Corp.
923 McBurney Dr.
Lebanon, OH 45036

All scripture quotations are from the King James Bible (public domain).

Cover Design Concept and Internal Graphics by the author.
Cover Design Art Work and External Graphics by Kayla Lipot.

ISBN 13:	978-1-7349780-0-1
ISBN 10:	1-7349780-0-1
First Revision 10-2025

Technisys

To schedule author seminars, interviews,
or other speaking engagements,
go to: www.3woes.com
or write:
Technisys Corp.
923 McBurney Dr.
Lebanon, OH 45036

Technisys

THE THREE WOES

A
Guide to Understanding Revelation
and
End Time Prophecies

In The Three Woes, Revelation's Hidden pre-Trib Timeline will be revealed and then other prophecies will be examined to determine where we are in the prophetic timeline. God's Feast Days will be studied to determine their impact on the timing of the rapture. We will examine the mystery of the seven sealed book and the need for a Kinsman Redeemer.
We will also explore man's purpose in life and why man needs a savior.

Visit: www.3woes.com

The Three Woes
A Guide To Understanding Revelation and End Time Prophecies

*I dedicate this book to the memory of my Grandparents
and Great Grandparents,
and to the spiritual heritage they left me,
without which, this book never would have been written.*

Thank You.

The Three Woes
A Guide To Understanding Revelation and End Time Prophecies

TTW1

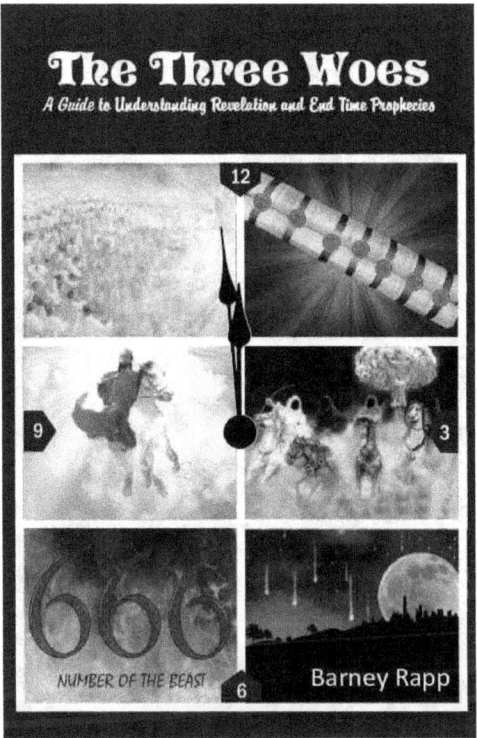

Book 1 introduces the reader to the scripture verse that is the key of how to read the Book of Revelation. Just as a good map provides a legend or key on how to read the map, the Book of Revelation provides a key showing how to read it. Following this the first book delves into a number of important basic theological concepts that are important to the study of end time prophecies such as:

- The Seven God ordained Feast Days
- Why Christ must return
- What is man's purpose in Life
- What is the Seven Sealed Book of Revelation

The Three Woes
A Guide To Understanding Revelation and End Time Prophecies

TTW2

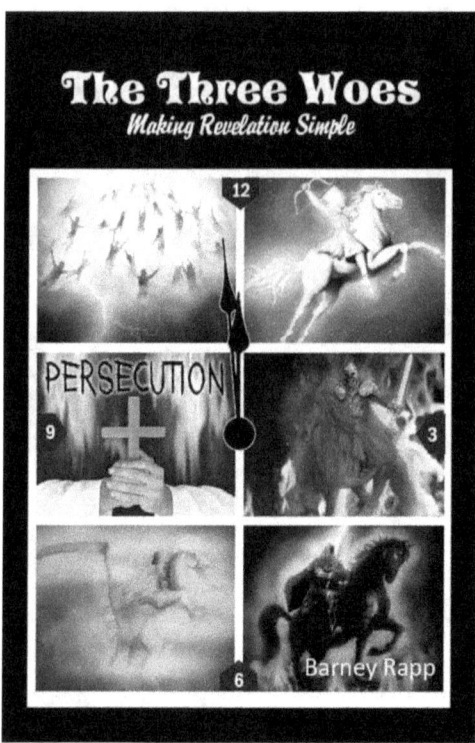

Book 2 begins building on the foundation established in Book 1 by proving the concept of a Transition Period. The book scripturally defines the term great tribulation and examines the correlation between the seals of Revelation and the signs of Matthew. Finally, the book examines each of the following post rapture time frames as shown below:

- Post Rapture Transition
- 1st Half of Daniel's Seventieth Week
- 2nd Half of Daniel's Seventieth Week
- Unraveling Mystery Babylon
- The timing of Ezekiel's War

The Three Woes
A Guide To Understanding Revelation and End Time Prophecies

TTW3

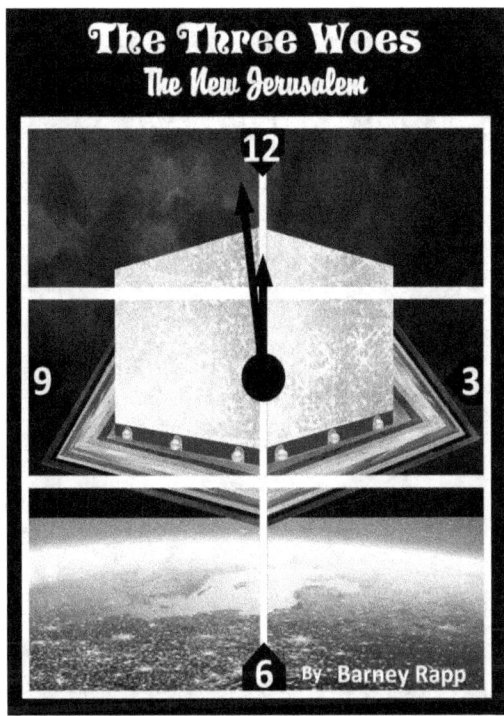

Book 3 picks up where Book 2 closes. It explores the physical and aesthetic characteristics of the Holy City while also addressing key doctrinal questions. Issues of importance for those who want to make heaven, the New Jerusalem, their home. Issues such as:

- What is man?
- What is a soul?
- What is the value of a soul?
- What happens at death?
- Where do we go after death?
- Where does the body go?
- Where does the spirit go?
- Where does the soul go?

The Three Woes
A Guide To Understanding Revelation and End Time Prophecies

TTW4

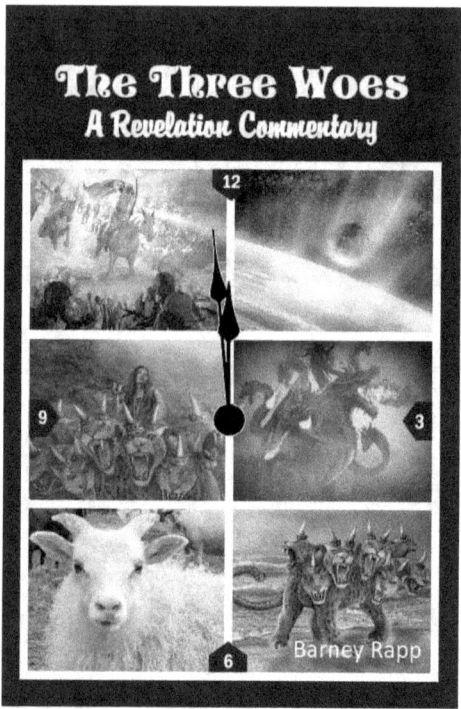

Book 4 is a commentary on the Book of Revelation. It is the fourth book in this series. It is a culmination of ten years of prayerful intensive study. The three woes are used to establish Revelation's timeline and the Book of Revelation is the primary source used to interpret its allegorical descriptions of the red dragon, the beast, the two horned Goat and the mysterious woman riding the beast. In this book we will answer the following questions:

- Who is the Red Dragon?
- Who is the Beast from the sea?
- Who is the Two Horned Goat?
- Who is Mystery Babylon?

The Three Woes
A Guide To Understanding Revelation and End Time Prophecies

Contents

Chapter One 1

  Introduction 1

    Following and Learning from the Begats 1

    Approaching the Book of Revelation 3

    Worksheet Questions for Chapter 1 5

Chapter Two 7

  Discovering Revelation's Timeline 7

    Analyzing Revelation 7

    Analyzing the Three Woes 9

    Examining the Activities of the Three Woes 13

    The Significance of the Second and Third Woes 15

    The Transition Period 17

    Additional Gleanings From The Three Woes 18

    Summary of Revelations Time Frames................................. 19

    The Rapture of the Church 20

    Worksheet Questions for Chapter 2 24

Chapter Three 27

  Major End Time Prophecies 27

    The First Prophecy 28

    The Second Prophecy 31

    The Third Prophecy 32

    The Fourth Prophecy 33

    The Fifth Prophecy 35

The Three Woes
A Guide To Understanding Revelation and End Time Prophecies

    The Sixth Prophecy 37

    The Seventh Prophecy 38

    The Eighth & Ninth Prophecy 39

    Summary 40

    Worksheet Questions for Chapter 3 42

Chapter Four 43

    Ezekiel's War 43

        The Countries of Ezekiel's War 45

        The Timing of Ezekiel's War 46

        Ezekiel's Visions 47

        Review of Ezekiel's Vision 51

        Israel Today 52

        Description of Ezekiel's War 53

        Worksheet Questions for Chapter 4 56

Chapter Five 59

    Are We Living in the End Times? 59

        The Olivet Discourse 59

        Deception 61

        Rumors of Wars and Wars 65

        Pestilences 66

        Earthquakes 66

        Afflictions 67

        Betrayals 67

        Forbidding To Marry 70

The Three Woes
A Guide To Understanding Revelation and End Time Prophecies

Calling Evil Good, and Good Evil 71

Worksheet Questions for Chapter 5 76

Chapter Six 77

  Understanding Revelation's Mysteries 77

    The First Four Seals - The Four Horsemen of the Apocalypse 79

    The Fifth Seal - Persecution 83

    The Sixth Seal 85

    The 144,000 of the Children of Israel.. 92

    The First Woe - The Locusts with a Scorpion Sting 93

    The Second Woe - The Two Witnesses 95

    The Third Woe - The Satanic Trinity 100

    Who Is The Antichrist 109

    Who Is The False Prophet 114

    Worksheet Questions for Chapter 6 119

Chapter Seven 123

  Fulfillment of the Feast Days 123

    The Passover - Christ's Death... 128

    The Feast of Unleavened Bread - Christ's Burial.......................... 129

    The Feast of First Fruits - Christ's Resurrection 131

    The Feast of Weeks - Giving of the Holy Spirit............................. 132

    The Feast of Trumpets - Christ Raptures His Church 133

    The Feast of Atonement - Christ's Return to Earth...................... 134

    The Feast of the Tabernacles - Christ's Millennial Reign 136

    No Man Knows the Day Nor Hour... 137

The Three Woes
A Guide To Understanding Revelation and End Time Prophecies

 Discerning the Time and Season 139

 Worksheet Questions for Chapter 7 142

Chapter Eight 145

 The Greatest Prophecy of All, The Return of Jesus Christ 145

  Why is the Fulfillment of this Prophecy so Necessary? 145

  The Need for a Savior 151

  The Blood Sacrifice 153

  We Need a Savior to Escape the Second Death 155

  Worksheet Questions for Chapter 8 161

Chapter Nine 163

 Post End Time Prophecies 163

  What is Man's Purpose in Life? 163

  The Saints of God, Future Judges 166

  The Conclusion of the Battle of Armageddon 171

  Post Millennial Reign 173

  Worksheet Questions for Chapter 9 176

Chapter Ten 179

 What Is the Seven Sealed Book of Revelation Chapter 5 179

  The Law of the Kinsman Redeemer 181

  Christ, Our Kinsman Redeemer 183

  Worksheet Questions for Chapter 10 188

Chapter Eleven 191

 Conclusion 191

  This Is Our Season 191

The Three Woes
A Guide To Understanding Revelation and End Time Prophecies

    The Ten Commandments 194

    Examining the Spiritual Health of Our Society 194

    Examining the Spiritual Health of the Church 199

    The Biblical Path Back to God 203

    Worksheet Questions for Chapter 11 206

Work Sheet Answers 207

    Worksheet Answers for Chapter 1 208

    Worksheet Answers for Chapter 2 211

    Worksheet Answers for Chapter 3 213

    Worksheet Answers for Chapter 4 215

    Worksheet Answers for Chapter 5 218

    Worksheet Answers for Chapter 6 220

    Worksheet Answers for Chapter 7 225

    Worksheet Answers for Chapter 8 227

    Worksheet Answers for Chapter 9 230

    Worksheet Answers for Chapter 10 232

    Worksheet Answers for Chapter 11 234

Biblical Lineage Charts 239

Study Material Resources 247

The Three Woes
A Guide To Understanding Revelation and End Time Prophecies

Chapter One
Introduction

Following and Learning from the Begats

In Genesis, one can easily see and follow the begats from generation to generation to establish specific times when certain events happened. For example, one can easily follow the lineage of Adam's descendants to establish that Noah's flood occurred 1656 years after the creation of Adam.

A study along this line can provide a wealth of insight that might otherwise be missed. Adam lived to the age of 930 years. Adam's grandson Enos was born when Adam was 235 years old, so he knew his grandfather for almost 700 years before Adam died. Noah was born 84 years before Enos died. That's a lifetime to us in our age. Imagine the history that Enos could have shared with Noah about Adam and Eve. How many stories were passed down about their life in the Garden of Eden and their life after they were cast out of the Garden of Eden?

There is another interesting concept that can be learned from a timeline study in Genesis. If you trace the lineages from Adam to Joseph, you will see that Joseph was sold into Egyptian bondage 2276 years after Adam was created. See table below.

Years from Creation	Timeline and Lineage According to Genesis and History	Gregorian Calendar	Jewish Calendar
0	Year Adam was Created	3761 BC	0
2276	Year Joseph was Sold into Slavery	1485 BC	2276

The Three Woes
A Guide To Understanding Revelation and End Time Prophecies

That brings us to about 400 years before the Jewish exodus from Egypt. Historians disagree, but generally place the Exodus somewhere between 500 BC and 1300 BC. Let's take 1085 BC as the year of the Exodus as shown in the table below.

Years from Creation	Timeline and Lineage According to Genesis and History	Gregorian Calendar	Jewish Calendar
0	Year Adam was Created	3761 BC	0
2276	Year Joseph was Sold into Slavery	1485 BC	2276
2676	Year the Jewish Bondage in Egypt ended – The Exodus	**1085 BC**	2676

If we use 1085 BC as the year of the Exodus and add 2259 years to it, the year of Joseph's birth, plus 17, his age when he was sold into bondage, plus 400, the years spent in captivity, and 2020, our current year and the years since Christ's birth, you get 5781, which is the current year according to the 2020 Jewish calendar.

Years from Creation	Timeline and Lineage According to Genesis and History	Gregorian Calendar	Jewish Calendar
0	Year Adam was Created	3761 BC	0
2276	Year Joseph was Sold into Slavery	1485 BC	2276
2676	Year the Jewish Bondage in Egypt ended – The Exodus	1085 BC	2676
3761	Year of Christ's Birth	0 BC	3761
5781	Years following Christ's Birth until 2020	2020 AD	**5781**

Chapter One
Introduction

This does two things, one, it supports the historic estimate of when the Jewish Exodus occurred and it supports the accuracy of the Jewish calendar. It also refutes the concept that man has been on the earth for millions of years.

Approaching the Book of Revelation

This raises the following question. Does Revelation have any timeline clues like Genesis? The answer is yes. However, Genesis is like walking down a dry creek bed and finding golden nuggets all over the place. All you need to do is reach down and pick them up. Revelation is more like using a pick and shovel to dig through a mountain side. The nuggets are there but you have to work to get to them. So, let's prepare ourselves to start digging in the Book of Revelation.

The ability to understand the Book of Revelation can be greatly affected by how we approach the book. Do we take it serious, is it a joke, is it a science fiction story, is it part truth and part false? Approaching it with a right attitude and understanding can greatly enhance our ability to understand what God is trying to tell us through John's Book of Revelation. Does that mean that we will be able to understand everything we read? Probably not! There will most likely be some written imagery and visual symbols that we may not fully understand until the time that they actually occur. But if we approach the reading of the Book of Revelation with a prayerful attitude, an open heart and an open mind, believing that it is God's Word given to us by Devine inspiration through John, then there is much we can learn.

Once we have a proper attitude, the next issue is determining how we should read the Book of Revelation? Is it a collection of

The Three Woes
A Guide To Understanding Revelation and End Time Prophecies

unrelated short stories like a Readers Digest? Is it a single story that jumps around? Does it have flashbacks? Does it jump forward and then backward? Does it contain multiple views of the same story? Is it one contiguous story from front to back?

We will start looking at these issues and searching for clues in the next chapter. As we said, Revelation doesn't have any lineages but if you dig through the book, there are some timeline clues to be found. Remember, initially we won't be focusing so much on the content and meaning of the symbolism of the Book of Revelation but searching for the timeline clues. The next chapter will be a more difficult read, but if you will see it through, it will be worth the effort.

Biblical Lineage Charts are at the back of this book.

Chapter One
Introduction

Worksheet Questions for Chapter 1

1. What was Enos' relationship to Adam?

2. How old was Adam when Enos celebrated his 30th birthday?

3. How old was Enos when Adam died?

4. What kind of stories do you think Adam might have shared with his grandson for the 600 plus years that he knew him as an adult?

5. How old was Enos when Noah celebrated his 30th birthday?

6. How old was Noah when Enos died?

The Three Woes
A Guide To Understanding Revelation and End Time Prophecies

7. What stories do you think Noah's grandparents and all other living great...grandparents through to Enos might have shared with Noah when he was an adult?

8. What was the name of the oldest man to ever live and how old was he when he died?

9. Where in the Bible does it tell us when Noah's flood occurred?

10. What year following Adam's creation was Joseph born? How did you calculate this date?

11. How old was Joseph when he stood before pharaoh?

12. According to the Hebrew Bible and the Jewish calendar, how long has man been on the earth?

Chapter Two
Discovering Revelation's Timeline

Analyzing Revelation

Can we look at the Book of Revelation and find any proof that it should be read in a chronological manner? In Genesis we are provided with the age of an individual such that we can assign dates from the beginning to nearly the end of the book. Is there any such mechanism in the Book of Revelation whereby we can prove that it should be read in a contiguous chronological manner as well? The salutation to each of the seven churches has been considered a historical representation of the church age, but although this may be true, it can't be proven. If we take a look at the seven seals however, we can clearly see that one seal is opened after another, clearly in a sequential or chronological order. The seventh seal is opened at Revelation 8:1 and since there is not an eighth seal, it is not immediately clear when the activities included within the opening of the seventh seal are complete. So how can we determine the duration or length of the seals, especially the seventh seal?

As we look at Chart 1 we can quickly see that the first four seals had a duration or span of only two verses each. We are given no clue as to the length of time that they might have spanned. We don't know if it was weeks, years or decades. The fifth seal is somewhat similar, it covers three verses but again we can't define a fixed time span to assign to it. All we can say for sure is that the fifth seal martyrs are growing impatient. Turning our attention to the sixth seal, we see that it encompasses the last six verses of Revelation Chapter 6 and all of Chapter 7. Once again we are not provided with any assigned time span. There is a lot that is taking

The Three Woes
A Guide To Understanding Revelation and End Time Prophecies

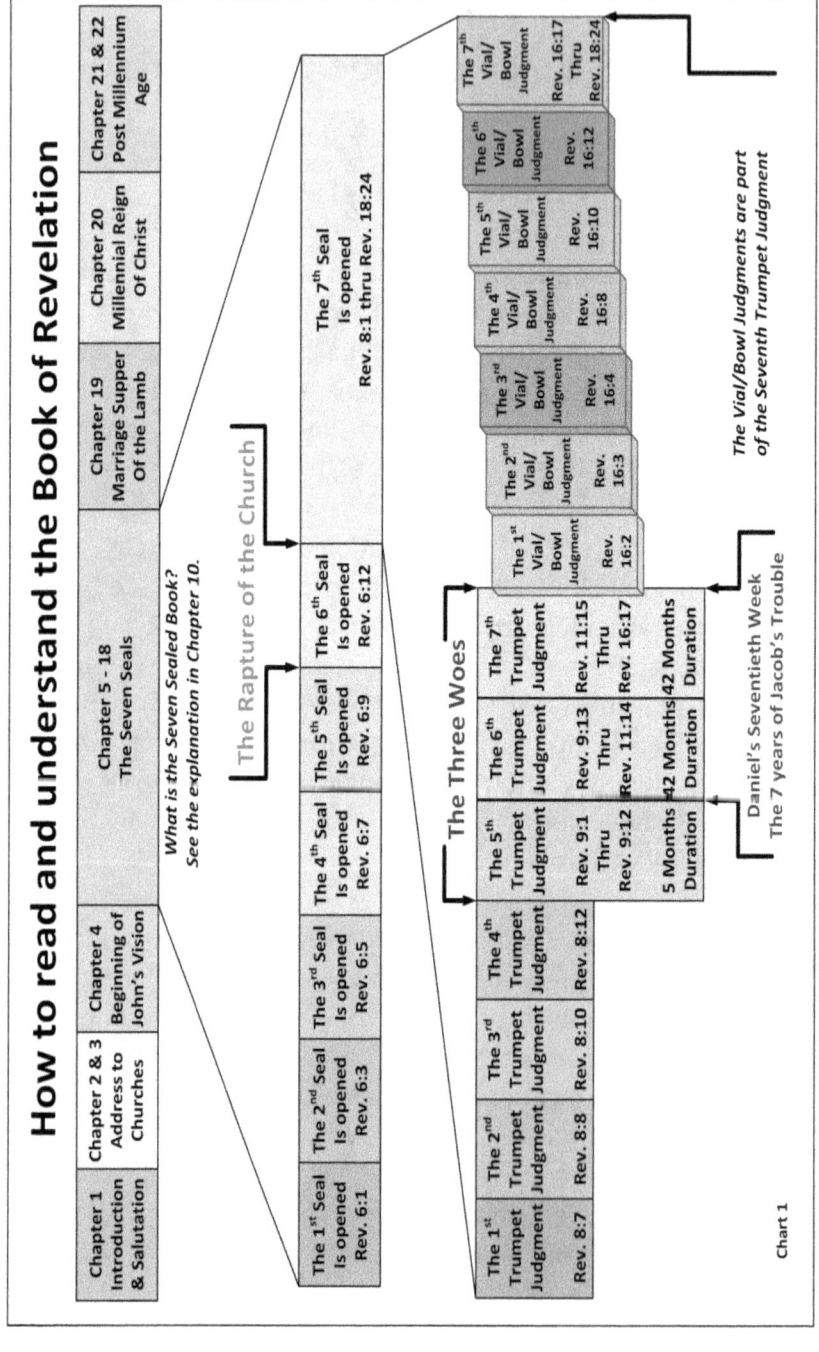

Chart 1

Chapter Two
Discovering Revelation's Timeline

place with the opening of the sixth seal. There is a great earthquake, changes to the sun and moon, stars fall, mountains and islands are physically moved, and all the people on earth cry out. We also see the sealing of the 144,000 children of Israel and we are introduced to a great multitude in heaven.

Thus far, as the seals have been opened, we have seen an increase in activity associated with the opening of each successive seal, especially the last one. In Revelation 8:1, the seventh seal is opened. This is the first seal where we are provided with a time span. The time span is one half hour, thirty minutes of silence. Are we to assume that 30 minutes of silence is the only time span assigned to this seal? Not at all. As we read on to Verse 2, we see seven trumpets being given to seven angels. This is the beginning of the trumpet judgments associated with the seventh seal.

Looking at the first four trumpet judgments, we see a parallel to the first seals, the first two trumpet judgments only span one verse each and the third and fourth trumpet judgments span only three verses each. Once again none of these judgments provide a span of time to be associated with them. **What we do see is that the seals and also the trumpet judgments appear as though they are being opened one at a time and in sequential order.** In Revelation Chapters 6 and 8, the seals aren't opened all at once, but one at a time and in Revelation Chapter 8 the trumpet angels don't sound all at once, but one at a time.

Analyzing the Three Woes

After the sounding of the fourth Trumpet Judgment Angel, we come to Revelation 8:13 which is the key to understanding how to read Revelation. This verse hides a timeline that is buried within the Book of Revelation, revealing the key to reading and understanding this magnificent mystery. Just like a map provides a legend or key to explain how to read it, Revelation 8:13 is the key to understanding how to read this mysterious book.

> **Revelation Time Lines Found in the Three Woes**
>
> **Rev. 8:13**
> Woe, woe, woe to the inhabiters of the earth because of the three angels yet to sound.

As we look at this verse, we see an angel flying in the midst of heaven and declaring a proclamation. As we casually read the proclamation, it seems this angel is just being emotionally expressive when he says, "Woe, woe, woe to the inhabiters of the earth." But what is so easily missed here is the fact that this angel is connecting these three woes to the remaining three Trumpet Judgment Angels who are yet to sound. If we are aware enough to make this connection, then there are hidden nuggets of truth and understanding buried for us in the next eight chapters of Revelation.

There's the problem. Most of us don't sit down and read eight chapters of Revelation all at once. Thus far, we have become accustomed to seeing the activities of the seals and trumpet angels span only a few verses. But now, that is about to change. To truly understand the message of this one verse we must consider the content of the next eight chapters. The content and structure of the next eight chapters will become our foundational blueprint for the prophetic story that John began laying out for us beginning in Chapter 4.

Chapter Two
Discovering Revelation's Timeline

The best way to find this foundational structure is to begin reading at Revelation 9:1 as though we are on a treasure hunt. You will find that Revelation 9:1 announces the sounding of the fifth Trumpet Angel which turns out to be the beginning of the first woe. Continue reading as you search for a statement indicating that the first woe is finished. Don't worry about any other content, we will consider it later. For now, just read, searching for the end of the first woe. You will find this at Revelation 9:12. Make note of these break points. They are our first nuggets.

Notice that at the very next verse, Revelation 9:13, we are told that the sixth angel has sounded. Make note of this and again continue reading as you search for a statement indicating that the second woe is finished. You will find a statement announcing that the second woe is past at Revelation 11:14. Record this break point and notice that at the next verse, Revelation 11:15, you will find the sounding of the seventh Trumpet Angel. Our search now becomes a little tricky. As we read to the end of the Book of Revelation, we do not find a statement indicating the third woe is past. However, what we do find are the words "It is done." This declaration is found at Revelation 16:17. Be sure to record this as the last break point.

This phrase, "It is done," indicates three things: (1) the seventh Vial/Bowl Angel has poured out his Vial/Bowl judgment upon the earth, (2) with this pouring out, the sounding of the seventh Trumpet Angel is finished and the third woe is past, and (3) the impact or effect of the opening of the seventh seal is also complete. The pouring out of God's wrath upon the earth and mankind is now finished even though John is not yet finished with telling us about its impact.

Verse	Defining Activity
Rev. 9:1	5th Trumpet Angel Sounds starting 1st Woe
Rev. 9:12	1st Woe is past
Rev. 9:13	6th Trumpet Angel Sounds starting 2nd Woe
Rev. 11:14	2nd Woe is past
Rev. 11:15	7th Trumpet Angel Sounds starting 3rd Woe
Rev. 16:17	"It is done," the third Woe is past

Chapter Two
Discovering Revelation's Timeline

At this point you should have a table that resembles the one above. As we view this table we should have an epiphany. The first thing we should recognize is that God's Word is confirming that the activities from Revelation 9:1 through Revelation 16:17 are sequential. There are no flashbacks and there is no jumping forward in time anywhere. It should be obvious that not only are these last three Trumpet Angels sounding in sequential order, but so are the first four. Not only that, but since the Trumpet Angels came out of the opening of the seventh seal, it becomes obvious that the seven seals were also opened in sequential order.

The next question we should be asking ourselves is whether God provided us with any time frames that can be assigned to any of these three woes. To answer this question, we will need to read from Revelation 9:1 through Revelation 16:17 once again. This time, instead of searching for the beginning and ending of a woe, we are now searching for prophetic activities that have specific time frames assigned to them. The results of our search can be found in the three tables below. There is one table for each woe.

Examining the Activities of the Three Woes

The first woe, which corresponds to the fifth trumpet judgment angel, had one prophetic event which had an assigned timeframe. That event told us that locusts would torment men for five months.

First Woe	
Verse	Defining Activity
Rev. 9:1	5th Trumpet Angel Sounds starting 1st Woe
Rev. 9:2-5	Locusts from bottomless pit have power to torment men five months
Rev. 9:12	1st Woe is past

The Three Woes
A Guide To Understanding Revelation and End Time Prophecies

The second woe corresponds to the sixth trumpet judgment angel. This woe has two prophetic events, each with an assigned timeframe. One event was the gentiles controlling the holy city for forty two months and the other event was the two witnesses prophesying for forty two months. Most of us correctly associate the two witnesses with the first one half of the Seven Years of Jacob's Trouble. So, are these two prophecies happening sequentially or simultaneously? To accurately answer that question we will need to look at the prophecies of the third woe.

Second Woe	
Verse	Defining Activity
Rev. 9:13	6th Trumpet Angel Sounds starting 2nd Woe
Rev. 11:2-3	The holy city shall be tread under foot by the Gentiles for forty-two months Time Frame = 42 months = 1260 days
Rev. 11:7	Two witnesses given power to prophesy for a thousand two hundred and three score days Time Frame = 1260 days
Rev. 11:14	2nd Woe is past

Third Woe	
Verse	Defining Activity
Rev. 11:15	7th Trumpet Angel Sounds starting 3rd Woe
Rev. 12:6	The woman flees to the wilderness for a thousand two hundred and three score days Time Frame = 1260 days
Rev. 12:13-14	The serpent persecutes the woman for a time, and times and half a time Time Frame = 3.5 years = 1260 days
Rev. 13:1-7	The beast makes war with the saints for forty- two months Time Frame = 42 months = 1260 days
Rev. 16:17	It is done, the third Woe is past

Chapter Two
Discovering Revelation's Timeline

The third woe corresponds to the seventh trumpet judgment angel. This angel has three prophetic events each with an assigned timeframe. One was the woman, Israel, fleeing to the wilderness for forty-two months. The second was the dragon persecuting the woman for forty-two months. The third was the antichrist making war against the saints for forty-two months.

The second woe had two forty-two month long prophecies. If they were sequential they could potentially be a match for the Seven Years of Jacob's Trouble. However, when we consider the third woe with its three forty-two month long prophecies we are pointed to a new interpretation. Taking the second and third woes together there are a total of five forty-two month long timeframes. Taken sequentially, that comes to a total of seventeen and one-half years. However, if the prophecies occur simultaneously within their respective woes, then we suddenly have a seven year timeframe whose prophecies are a direct match for the Seven Years of Jacob's Trouble.

The Significance of the Second and Third Woes

As we just stated, if the prophecies of the second woe occur simultaneously and the prophecies of the third woe also occur simultaneously then we may have just discovered Daniel's Seventieth Week. Could this be? The answer is yes! As we look at the Angelic Proclamations for the second woe in the top half of the chart on the next page, we see three prophecies that are presented to John in sequential order. The angel is only able to present one prophecy at a time to John, and John is only able to tell us about one prophecy at a time. Therefore, we can only read about one prophecy at a time. Thus, the prophecies seem to be happening sequentially even though they are actually simultaneous events as shown in the Resulting Punishment

The Three Woes
A Guide To Understanding Revelation and End Time Prophecies

	Angelic Proclamation			Resulting Punishment	
Fifth Angel	Rev. 9:1 And the fifth angel sounded	Rev. 9:2-5 Locusts torment men five months	Rev. 9:12 One woe is past.	**1st Woe**	Rev. 9:2-5 Locusts from the bottomless pit have power to torment men 5 months	Five Months
Sixth Angel	Rev. 9:13 And the sixth angel sounded	Rev. 9:14-15 Angels kill mankind	Rev. 11:2-3 Holy City taken	Rev. 11:3-12 Two witnesses	Rev. 11:14 The second woe is past	**2nd Woe**	Rev. 9:14-15 Four angels from Euphrates river to slay a third of men for an hour, and a day, and a month and a year	Rev. 11:2-3 The holy city shall be tread under foot by the gentiles for forty two months	Rev. 11:3-12 My two witnesses shall prophesy a thousand two hundred and three score days	3.5 years
Seventh Angel	Rev. 11:15 The seventh angel sounded	Rev. 12:6 Woman flees to wilderness	Rev. 12:13-14 Serpent persecutes woman	Rev. 13:1-7 The beast makes war with the saints	Rev. 16:17 It is done. (3rd Woe past)	**3rd Woe**	Rev. 12:6 The woman flees to the wilderness for a thousand two hundred and three score days.	Rev. 12:13-14 The serpent (dragon) persecutes the woman for a time, and times and half a time	Rev. 13:1-7 The beast makes war with the saints for forty two months and over comes them	3.5 years

Rev. 8:13 Woe, woe, woe to the inhabiters of the earth because of the three angels yet to sound.

The Seven Years of Jacob's Trouble

Chart 4

Chapter Two
Discovering Revelation's Timeline

portion of the bottom half of the chart. The same holds true for the three prophecies associated with the third woe. After reviewing these six prophecies, they confirm that these events match the events associated with the Seven Years of Jacob's Trouble.

The Transition Period

If we look at Bible history, we notice that there was a Transition Period as mankind moved from the Prediluvian Age to the Postdiluvian Age and we will also find that there was a transition from the Age of the Prophets to the Church Age. The chart on the previous page is clearly capturing a time frame of seven years and five months as described in the Book of Revelation. Additionally, Revelation 6:1 through 8:12 tells us about the opening of six other seals as well as the sounding of four other trumpet judgment angels. Many students of the Bible have referred to this timeframe as The Tribulation Period or Great Tribulation. Since a portion of this timeframe actually begins prior to the rapture of the Church and because many of us associate the term tribulation to a time frame of seven years, a better term for this period of time would be the Transition Period. We are currently experiencing the transition from the Church Age to the Kingdom Age.

The Seven Years of Jacob's Trouble is clearly depicted in the chart on the previous page. The chart assigns 3.5 years to the 2nd woe and 3.5 years to the 3rd woe. The Bible also calls this timeframe Daniel's Seventieth Week. The church world has come to call this timeframe "The Great Tribulation." However, the term "The Great Tribulation" is not Biblically accurate. When Christ was addressing the church of Thyatira, He said He would cast her into Great Tribulation. Scripturally, the term tribulation means trouble directed toward the church. Since this was a church in John's time, Christ was obviously not referring to Daniel's Seventieth Week. Instead Christ was referring to a great time of trouble that would come upon the church of Thyatira. Throughout these writings, we will use one of two Biblical terms for this seven-year time frame. Those terms are Daniel's Seventieth Week and the Seven Years of Jacob's Trouble.

> *Behold, I will cast her into a bed, and them that commit adultery with her into great tribulation, except they repent of their deeds.*
> **Revelation 2:22 KJV**

Additional Gleanings From The Three Woes

The three woes define a period of time which begins at Revelation 8:13 and continues until Revelation 16:17. The duration of this time frame is seven years and five months. The three woes are sequential but some of the activities within the second and third woes are happening simultaneously even though John presents them to us in a sequential manner.

There are two major concepts that we should learn from the three woes.

First, the prophetic activities associated with the second and third woes are a perfect match for what we know will occur during the first and second half of the Seven Years of Jacob's Trouble. The Seven Years of Jacob's Trouble is a time that many of us have referred to as the great tribulation.

Second, if everything from Revelation Chapter 9:1 through Revelation 16:17 is sequential in nature, then might we infer that

Chapter Two
Discovering Revelation's Timeline

everything from the opening of the first seal at Revelation 6:1 through the sounding of the fourth trumpet judgment angel at Revelation 8:12 is also sequential in nature?

Chapter 6 of Revelation starts off with the opening of the first seal at Verse 1 and culminates with the opening of the sixth seal at Verses 12 through 17. We then see the opening of the seventh seal at Revelation 8:1. The first four trumpet judgment angels then sound later in Chapter 8 which brings us to the three woes at the end of Chapter 8. This seems to confirm a sequential set of activity from Revelation 6:1 through Revelation 16:17.

Be aware however, that the seventh seal is ended at Revelation 16:17 but as we study Revelation, we see that the description of the seventh trumpet judgment runs from Revelation 11:15 through Revelation 19:21. So in reality, the completion or conclusion of all of the consequences of the seventh trumpet and the opening of the seventh seal are not concluded until Revelation 19:21.

Looking at the activities of the three woes, we can begin to decipher the time frames of the book of Revelation and assemble the layout of the activities in the Book of Revelation as found back in Chart 1.

Summary of Revelations Time Frames

Some students of the Book of Revelation attempt to try and squeeze the opening of the seven seals, the seven trumpet judgments and the seven vial judgments into one seven year time frame that we understand to be Daniels' Seventieth Week. They do this by various means, either saying the story jumps around, or there are different views of the same occurrence, or that the narrative jumps around and is not contiguous. But we have just shown that the scripture clearly defines a contiguous period of seven years and five months that span from Revelation 9:1 through Revelation 16:17. We already have five months more than the seven years of Daniel's Seventieth Week and we haven't accounted for Revelation 5:1 through Revelation 8:13 yet.

So what is the problem, what do we do? Is there an error in the scripture? God forbid! What do we do now that we have established that the Book of Revelation should be read and studied and understood in a contiguous chronological manner?

The Rapture of the Church

Many theologians base the rapture of the church on three words spoken to John in Revelation 4:1. Those words are "come up hither." It should be pointed out that these three words were spoken to John, not to the church. John says the words were spoken to him to come up hither. When Lazarus died, Jesus specifically called to Lazarus to come forth. No one else came forth only Lazarus. It should also be noted that the same three words "come up hither" were spoken to the two witnesses in Revelation 11:12. The two witnesses were told to come up hither. Here again, only the two witnesses were caught up and no one else.

So if the rapture of the church doesn't occur at Revelation Chapter 4:1, then where might it occur? A much more logical time and place for the Rapture of the church is at the opening of the sixth seal at Revelation Chapter 6:12.

Further proof that the rapture of the church occurs at the end of Revelation Chapter 6 is provided by Jesus Himself. If we look at

Chapter Two
Discovering Revelation's Timeline

Matthew 24:27-31 we see Jesus clearly describing His return to the earth to rapture His church. The portion of scripture here that so clearly ties this event to Revelation Chapter 6:12 is what is called the Cosmic Signs. The Cosmic Signs are the darkening of the sun and moon and the stars of heaven fall. When we look at Revelation 6:12 & 13 we see the same Cosmic Signs.

> *For as the lightning cometh out of the east, and shineth even unto the west; so shall also the coming of the Son of man be. 28 For wheresoever the carcase is, there will the eagles be gathered together. 29 Immediately after the tribulation of those days shall the sun be darkened, and the moon shall not give her light, and the stars shall fall from heaven, and the powers of the heavens shall be shaken: 30 And then shall appear the sign of the Son of man in heaven: and then shall all the tribes of the earth mourn, and they shall see the Son of man coming in the clouds of heaven with power and great glory. 31 And he shall send his angels with a great sound of a trumpet, and they shall gather together his elect from the four winds, from one end of heaven to the other.*
> **Matthew 24:27-31 KJV**

> *And I beheld when he had opened the sixth seal, and, lo, there was a great earthquake; and the sun became black as sackcloth of hair, and the moon became as blood; 13 13 And the stars of heaven fell unto the earth, even as a fig tree casteth her untimely figs, when she is shaken of a mighty wind.*
> **Revelation 6:12-13 KJV**

So, if the church was not raptured at Chapter 4:1 but instead it was raptured at the opening of the sixth seal, then the great end time revival that some theologians attribute to Revelation 7:9 is actually a picture of the raptured church now in heaven. This would debunk the modern day concept that you can live however you want and get saved after the rapture has taken place.

> *Let no man deceive you by any means: for that day shall not come, except there come a falling away first, and that man of sin be revealed, the son of perdition;*
> **2 Thessalonians 2:3 KJV**

The reality of what it will be like on earth following the rapture of the church can be seen in Revelation 6:15-17.

> *And the kings of the earth, and the great men, and the rich men, and the chief captains, and the mighty men, and every bondman, and every free man, hid themselves in the dens and in the rocks of the mountains; 16 And said to the mountains and rocks, Fall on us, and hide us from the face of him that sitteth on the throne, and from the wrath of the Lamb: 17 For the great day of his wrath is come; and who shall be able to stand?*
> **Revelation 6:15-17 KJV**

A more in depth look at the opening of the sixth seal and why it is the rapture of the church will be covered later in the sixth chapter of this book as we take a much closer look at the sixth seal.

Chapter Two
Discovering Revelation's Timeline

Start	Rev. 9:1	And the fifth *trumpet* angel sounded	
	Rev. 9:2-5	Locusts from the bottomless pit have power to torment men five months	
Stop	Rev. 9:12	One woe is past	
Start	Rev. 9:13	And the sixth *trumpet* angel sounded	
	Rev. 9:14-15	The sixth angel loosed four angels from Euphrates river to slay a third of men for an hour, and a day, and a month and a year	*A point in time*
	Rev. 11:2-3	The holy city shall be tread under foot by the Gentiles for forty two months	*These times coincide with one another*
		Two witnesses given power to prophesy for a thousand two hundred and three score days	
	Rev. 11:7	The two witnesses complete their prophesy and are killed by the beast that is described by the seventh *trumpet* angel.	
Stop	Rev. 11:14	The second woe is past	
Start	Rev. 11:15	The seventh *trumpet* angel sounded	
	Rev. 12:1-3	A woman (Israel) appears in heaven - A great red dragon appears in heaven	
	Rev. 12:6	The woman (Israel) flees to the wilderness for a thousand two hundred and three score days	
	Rev. 12:12	Woe to the inhabiters of the earth	
	Rev. 12:13-14	The serpent (*dragon*) persecutes the woman for a time, and times and half a time	*These times will coincide*
	Rev. 13:1-7	The beast makes war with the saints for forty two months and over comes them. These saints are the Israeli people who turned to God through the ministry of the two witnesses and the 144,000 sealed children of Israel.	
Stop	Rev. 16:17	It is done	

Chart 2

The Three Woes
A Guide To Understanding Revelation and End Time Prophecies

Worksheet Questions for Chapter 2

1. What are the seven divisions of the Book of Revelation?

2. What are the three Woes of Revelation 8:13?

3. Where in Revelation does the 5th Trumpet Angel sound?

4. How do we know when the 5th Trumpet Angel has finished sounding?

5. What is the very next thing we see happening?

6. How do we know when the 7th Trumpet Angel finishes sounding?

Chapter Two
Discovering Revelation's Timeline

7. How much time is accounted for between the sounding of the 5th Trumpet Angel and when the 7th Trumpet Angel finishes sounding?

8. Where in Revelation do we see a picture of the rapture of the church taking place?

9. What evidence do you see that indicates that we probably won't instantaneously go from the church age into the tribulation period?

The Three Woes
A Guide To Understanding Revelation and End Time Prophecies

Chapter Three
Major End Time Prophecies

A few years ago, Hollywood produced a weekly series called "Early Edition." In this show, the star received tomorrow's newspaper today. What would you do if tomorrow's paper came to your door today? If you knew that you were going to die? Be lucky in love, unlucky in life? Who wouldn't like to know what the stock market is going to do, or whether you're going to get that job? Whether or not you believe in the Bible and in Bible prophecy, you probably have an interest in knowing what the future holds. Being in the know is never negative, it can be very empowering.

Many believe the Bible and many dismiss it, but one prophecy the Bible predicted was that the country of Israel would be re-established in the end times. Some would claim that this is just a chance prediction. The country of Israel was conquered by the Assyrians in 722 BC and 100 years later by the Babylonian Empire. Ultimately the people were dispersed around the world more than two millennia ago and their language lost. Then, in 1948 the people began to return to the Middle East and the country of Israel was re-established. Their Hebrew language was restored during the 19th century and into the 20th century. What an amazing coincidence if not a fulfillment of prophecy.

So the real test to see if this is a coincidence or a fulfilled prophecy, would be to see if there are any other prophecies, and have those prophecies been fulfilled or are they about to be fulfilled. After searching the scriptures of the major and Minor Prophets in the Bible, there are a number of prophecies that fall into this category. Part of these prophecies appear to have been fulfilled and one may be close to fulfillment. That leaves a few other prophecies for possible future fulfillment. Let's take a look at those prophecies now.

The Three Woes
A Guide To Understanding Revelation and End Time Prophecies

The First Prophecy

Keep not thou silence, O God: hold not thy peace, and be not still, O God. 2 For, lo, thine enemies make a tumult: and they that hate thee have lifted up the head. 3 They have taken crafty counsel against thy people, and consulted against thy hidden ones. 4 They have said, Come, and let us cut them off from being a nation; that the name of Israel may be no more in remembrance.
Psalm 83:1-4 KJV

For several thousand years now, there has been extreme conflict between the Jewish people and the people of the Arab Muslim world. After the destruction of the Jewish nation by the Assyrians and the Babylonians the conflict seemed to dissipate as the Jewish people were dispersed around the world. But since the establishment of the Jewish nation in 1948, the Arab Muslim world has ferociously and viciously renewed its' conflict with Israel. After the western world established the nation of Israel following WWII, the Israelis spent ten months defending themselves against a coalition of Arab states who were determined to destroy the young nation. The 1950s and early 1960s saw constant fedayeen incursions during which Arab guerillas infiltrated from Syria, Egypt, and Jordan into Israel, to carry out attacks against Israeli civilians and soldiers. Israel would respond with numerous reprisal operations carried out by the Israeli Defense Forces.

Prior to the 1967 Six-Day War, President Nasser of Egypt made the following statement, *"Our aim is the full restoration of the rights of the Palestinian people. In other words, we aim at the destruction of the State of Israel. The immediate aim: perfection of Arab military might. The national aim: the eradication of Israel."*

Chapter Three
Major End Time Prophecies

These words were uttered on November 18, 1965. They were the first in a long list of utterances against the new Jewish nation.

The Cairo Radio in Egypt broadcasted the following statements: on May 19, 1967: *"This is our chance Arabs, to deal Israel a mortal blow of annihilation, to blot out its entire presence in our holy land.,"* and on May 22, 1967: *"The Arab people is firmly resolved to wipe Israel off the map.",* and on May 27, 1967: *"We challenge you, Eshkol, to try all your weapons. Put them to the test; they will spell Israel's death and annihilation."*

On May 28, 1967, President Nasser said, *"We will not accept any ... coexistence with Israel. ... Today the issue is not the establishment of peace between the Arab states and Israel .... The war with Israel is in effect since 1948."*

On May 20, 1967, the Syrian Defense Minister Hafez Assad said, *"Syria's forces are "ready not only to repulse the aggression, but to initiate the act of liberation itself, and to explode the Zionist presence in the Arab homeland. The Syrian army, with its finger on the trigger, is united.... I as a military man, believe that the time has come to enter into a battle of annihilation"."*

On May 31, 1967, the President of Iraq, Abdel Rahman Aref made the following statement, *"The existence of Israel is an error which must be rectified. This is our opportunity to wipe out the ignominy which has been with us since 1948. Our goal is clear – to wipe Israel off the map. We shall, God willing, meet in Tel Aviv and Haifa."*

In June of 1967 the Six-Day War began. Its occurrence shouldn't have been much of a surprise considering so many Arab leaders were repeatedly threatening Israel with annihilation. But the threats of annihilation didn't end with this war. On December 11,

The Three Woes
A Guide To Understanding Revelation and End Time Prophecies

2006, at the International Conference to Review the Global Vision of the Holocaust, a gathering of Holocaust deniers in Tehran, President Ahmadinejad of Iran said: *"Thanks to people's wishes and God's will the trend for the existence of the Zionist regime is [headed] downwards and this is what God has promised and what all nations want. The Zionist regime will be wiped out soon the same way the Soviet Union was, and humanity will achieve freedom."*

In 2008, on Israel's 60th birthday, President Ahmadinejad of Iran said: *"Those who think they can revive the stinking corpse of the usurping and fake Israeli regime by throwing a birthday party are seriously mistaken. Today the reason for the Zionist regime's existence is questioned, and this regime is on its way to annihilation."*

In July 2012, ahead of Qods Day, President Ahmadinejad said that *"any freedom lover and justice seeker in the world must do its best for the annihilation of the Zionist regime in order to pave the path for the establishment of justice and freedom in the world,"*

In August 2012, at an annual protest against the existence of Israel, Iranian President Mahmoud Ahmadinejad said that *"the very existence of the Zionist regime is an insult to humanity"* and that *"the Zionist regime and the Zionists are a cancerous tumor."*

In February 2020, Mohsen Rezaee adviser to Iran's Khamenei said that "We would raze Tel Aviv to the ground for sure. We have been looking for such a pretext," according to a translation from the Middle East Media Research Institute. He added that "if they [the US] do something, we can use it as a pretext to attack Israel."

After reading all these quotes, it appears that this prophecy has been repeatedly fulfilled over the past several decades. In fact,

Chapter Three
Major End Time Prophecies

Israel is under such tremendous threats of attack and assault from terrorists that they have commissioned to build approximately 430 miles of concrete walls to protect themselves. There is prophetic importance to these protective barriers. The prophet Ezekiel said in Ezekiel 38:11 KJV *"I will go up to the land of unwalled villages;."* This is a future prophecy that indicates that there will be a time somewhere in Israel's future when they will not be living behind walls. One could then reason that prior to the fulfillment of this prophecy, Israel was living behind protective walls. We will see the importance of understanding this later.

The Second Prophecy

And I will set the Egyptians against the Egyptians: and they shall fight every one against his brother, and every one against his neighbour; city against city, and kingdom against kingdom. 3 And the spirit of Egypt shall fail in the midst thereof; and I will destroy the counsel thereof: and they shall seek to the idols, and to the charmers, and to them that have familiar spirits, and to the wizards.
Isaiah 19:2-3 KJV

Let's take a look at the political landscape of Egypt over the past 90 years. Egypt was under British rule for the forty years prior to 1922. In 1922, following the Unilateral Declaration of Egyptian Independence by the United Kingdom, the Kingdom of Egypt was established. The Muslim Brotherhood was founded in Egypt in 1928 as an Islamist religious, political, and social movement. During the 1930's the Brotherhood developed links to the Nazis which lasted through the end of World War II. Through the second half of the 1940s there were many bombings and assassination attempts and in December of 1948 Egypt's prime minister was assassinated by Brotherhood member Abdel Meguid Ahmed Hassan. The government of Egypt ordered the dissolution of the Brotherhood. In 1952, members of the Muslim Brotherhood were accused of taking part in arson that destroyed approximately 750 buildings in downtown Cairo. In 1954 Gamal 'Abd al-Nasser abolished the Brotherhood after an assassination attempt on his life. Nasser imprisoned and punished thousands of Brotherhood members. In 1965 the Brotherhood executed a plot to overthrow the government and to assassinate the President and other Egyptian officials and personalities. In 1970 Anwar Sadat became President of Egypt and eased up on the ban of the Brotherhood but he was then assassinated in 1981 by an Islamic group with ties to the Brotherhood. In 1981 Hosni Mubarak became president and remained in power until the Egyptian revolution of 2011. Following the revolution, the Brotherhood emerged as the most powerful group in Egypt and Mohamed Morsi, a member of the Muslim Brotherhood became president until his overthrow in 2013. So what we see is a sixty plus year struggle pitting Egyptian against Egyptian.

The Third Prophecy

And the Egyptians will I give over into the hand of a cruel lord; and a fierce king shall rule over them, saith the Lord, the Lord of hosts.
Isaiah 19:4 KJV

The Arab Spring was a revolutionary wave of demonstrations and protests that turned into riots and civil wars in several countries of the Arab world. The Egyptian revolution drew much of its momentum from the Arab Spring. In February of 2011 the revolution left the Brotherhood in control of Egypt. The Brotherhood was legalized and they formed the Freedom and Justice Party. The new party rejected the candidacy of women and Coptic Christians for Egypt's presidency. The party won almost half the seats in the 2011–12 parliamentary election and

Chapter Three
Major End Time Prophecies

Mohammed Morsi, a member of the Muslim Brotherhood, won the 2012 presidential election. Morsi was elected as a democratic president, but after he was elected, he granted himself unlimited powers and the power to legislate without judicial oversight or review of his acts. He claimed that he would "protect" the nation from the Mubarak-era power structure, which he called "remnants of the old regime." Morsi issued an Islamist-backed draft constitution and called for a referendum, an act that his opponents called an "Islamist coup." These issues, along with complaints of prosecutions of journalists and attacks on nonviolent demonstrators, brought hundreds of thousands of protesters to the streets in 2012 protesting against the Egyptian president. The violence escalated rapidly and led to the deaths of over 600 people and injury of some 4,000, the worst mass killing in Egypt's modern history. In response to the protests, Morsi was eventually removed from power by the military. So it seems that the democratically elected president was so cruel and evil that his rule was very short lived.

The Fourth Prophecy

And the waters shall fail from the sea, and the river shall be wasted and dried up. 6 And they shall turn the rivers far away; and the brooks of defence shall be emptied and dried up: the reeds and flags shall wither.
Isaiah 19:5-6 KJV

The Aswan Dam in southern Egypt is really two dams. The first of the two is called the Aswan Low Dam and was completed in 1902. The second dam is called the Aswan High Dam, it was completed in 1970. Before the second dam was built, the Nile River flooded every year during late summer. Due to the absence of appreciable rainfall, Egypt's agriculture depends entirely on irrigation. These floods brought high water with natural nutrients and minerals and in extreme high-water years the whole crop might be wiped out, while in low-water years widespread drought and famine occasionally occurred. As Egypt's population grew and conditions changed, the country needed the ability to control the floods, and thus these two dams were built. With the reservoir storage provided by the Aswan dams, the floods could be lessened and the water stored for later release. Sixteen hundred miles to the south in Ethiopia another dam is being built. This new dam was originally called the Millennium Dam but is now called the Grand Renaissance Dam. It is being built on the Blue Nile, the largest tributary to the Nile River.

From the very beginning, this relentless project has put Ethiopia at odds with Egypt. A war between Ethiopia and Egypt nearly erupted during the brief reign of former Egyptian president, Mohamed Morsi, whom we discussed in the last prophecy. He said that "Ethiopian blood" would substitute for every drop of lost water. Ethiopia began diverting water from the Nile River in May 2013 following Morsi's removal from office. This dam is currently scheduled to be completed sometime in 2022. Since the Grand Renaissance Dam has the capacity to store such a large volume of water, the dam will need to be filled over a period of several years.

Egypt and Ethiopia have been in heated discussions over the schedule for filling this dam for many years now. It's not surprising that it's not uncommon to see an article with headlines like the following on the internet.

"Will Ethiopia's Grand Renaissance Dam Dry the Nile in Egypt?"

In review, we have just finished looking at three distinct predictions concerning Egypt. They were found in just five verses of scripture, Isaiah 19:2-6. It appears as though it took

Chapter Three
Major End Time Prophecies

approximately ninety years for the conditions and circumstances to be put into place for the fulfillment of these prophecies. The first prophecy appears to have been fulfilled in 2011 and the second in 2012 while the third may be on the verge of being fulfilled.

The Fifth Prophecy

For they have consulted together with one consent: they are confederate against thee: 6 The tabernacles of Edom, and the Ishmaelites; of Moab, and the Hagarenes; 7 Gebal, and Ammon, and Amalek; the Philistines with the inhabitants of Tyre; 8 Assur also is joined with them: they have holpen the children of Lot. Selah. 9 Do unto them as unto the Midianites; as to Sisera, as to Jabin, at the brook of Kison: 10 Which perished at Endor: they became as dung for the earth. 11 Make their nobles like Oreb, and like Zeeb: yea, all their princes as Zebah, and as Zalmunna: 12 Who said, Let us take to ourselves the houses of God in possession. 13 O my God, make them like a wheel; as the stubble before the wind. 14 As the fire burneth a wood, and as the flame setteth the mountains on fire; 15 So persecute them with thy tempest, and make them afraid with thy storm. 16 Fill their faces with shame; that they may seek thy name, O Lord. 17 Let them be confounded and troubled for ever; yea, let them be put to shame, and perish: 18 That men may know that thou, whose name alone is JEHOVAH, art the most high over all the earth.
Psalm 83:5-18 KJV

We just finished looking at the first four verses of this chapter in Psalms when we reviewed a previous prophecy. As we continue studying this 83rd chapter of Psalms, the Psalm 83 War, remember how the last three prophecies we reviewed were found in contiguous verses of Isaiah Chapter 19. There are those who believe that this part of Psalm 83 has been fulfilled but there is also a large number who are still looking for its fulfillment. Whatever is true, as we look at the rhetoric and the mindset of the Arab countries surrounding Israel, it is obvious that the conditions still exist for the future fulfillment of this prophecy. We've seen the history of the Six-Day War, where the Arab nations surrounding Israel joined together and attacked Israel with an overwhelming force, only to see that force defeated in a seemingly miraculous six days. The Six-Day War may or may not have been the fulfillment of this prophecy but it does give us a good picture of what the fulfillment of this prophecy might look like. The October 7, 2023 attack on Israel by Hamas may well be a further fulfillment of this prophecy.

Modern Day Psalm 83 Countries

Ammon = **Palestinians & North Jordan**
Moab = **Palestinians & Central Jordan**
Edom = **Palestinians & South Jordan**
Gebal = **Hezbollah & North Lebanon**
Tyre = **Hezbollah & South Lebanon**
Ishmaelites = **Saudi Arabia**
Philistines = **Hamas of Gaza**
Assur = **Syria & North Iraq**
Hagarenes = **Egyptians**
Amalek = **Sinai**

Chapter Three
Major End Time Prophecies

The Sixth Prophecy

The burden of Damascus. Behold, Damascus is taken away from being a city, and it shall be a ruinous heap.
Isaiah 17:1 KJV

This is a very short and simple prophecy, but it is also a controversial prophecy. There are some who believe that this prophecy was fulfilled in 732BC. Others believe that it is yet to be fulfilled. When you study the history of Damascus, it lays claim to being one of the oldest continuously inhabited cities in the world. This is where many have a problem. People don't generally live in a "ruinous heap" and some versions translate this verse using the word "forever." While the King James translation above does not use the word "forever", it does seem to imply it. The verse does not say "Damascus is taken away from being a city, and it shall be rebuilt", it says, "Damascus is taken away from being a city, and it shall be a ruinous heap", implying that it will go on being a "ruinous heap."

Many cities in history have experienced both natural and man-made devastation. The devastation may have been a total or a near total destruction but the cities were rebuilt. Two of the most memorable of these were Hiroshima and Nagasaki. These cities were totally destroyed only to be rebuilt into marvelous modern metropolitan centers. It would seem that the scripture here is pronouncing a judgment against Damascus that would separate it from other cities of the world, again implying that Damascus will not be rebuilt following its destruction. As we have seen in the past, a nuclear weapon would certainly leave a "ruinous heap." The bombs dropped on Hiroshima and Nagasaki were 15 and 21 kilotons respectively. A modern nuclear weapon would be many times more powerful than those dropped on Hiroshima and Nagasaki. Today, the United States has weapons in the 9,000 and

21,000 kiloton range. That's as much as 1000 times larger than the Nagasaki bomb.

So how much damage might a bomb of this size cause? The melt down of the Chernobyl nuclear reactor is said to have released four hundred times more radioactive material than was released by the atomic bomb that was dropped on Hiroshima. The country of Ukraine has established an exclusion zone that is 38 miles in diameter around the Chernobyl nuclear plant and it is estimated that that area will not support life for another 20,000 years. Might this be the future for Damascus?

The current Syrian civil war began in the spring of 2011 and according to Wikipedia, the war has as many as 45 various factions or countries fighting for control. Many of these factions are enemies of Israel with one of those being Iran. For some time now, news agencies have been reporting on various clashes between some of these factions and the Israeli Defense Forces. It seems that these clashes could escalate very easily, with even a potential nuclear exchange when considered in light of the first prophecy.

The Seventh Prophecy

> *Therefore as I live, saith the Lord of hosts, the God of Israel, Surely Moab shall be as Sodom, and the children of Ammon as Gomorrah, even the breeding of nettles, and saltpits, and a perpetual desolation: the residue of my people shall spoil them, and the remnant of my people shall possess them.*
> **Zephaniah 2:9 KJV**

This seems like an insignificant prophecy but if the analysis of the above Damascus prophecy is accurate, then it could easily explain

Chapter Three
Major End Time Prophecies

how this prophecy could be fulfilled. If we look at a map of the Middle East, we can see that Damascus is north of Jordan and lies nearly parallel to the western border of Jordan. We have already found that Moab is the same as modern day central Jordan and Ammon is the area of northern Jordan. The prevailing trade winds in Damascus are from the north and the west. If Damascus is destroyed by a modern day nuclear weapon then the winds could indeed make northern and central Jordan a desolation.

The Eighth & Ninth Prophecy

In that day shall five cities in the land of Egypt speak the language of Canaan, and swear to the Lord of hosts; one shall be called, The city of destruction. 19 In that day shall there be an altar to the Lord in the midst of the land of Egypt, and a pillar at the border thereof to the Lord. 20 And it shall be for a sign and for a witness unto the Lord of hosts in the land of Egypt: for they shall cry unto the Lord because of the oppressors, and he shall send them a saviour, and a great one, and he shall deliver them. 21 And the Lord shall be known to Egypt, and the Egyptians shall know the Lord in that day, and shall do sacrifice and oblation; yea, they shall vow a vow unto the Lord, and perform it. 22 And the Lord shall smite Egypt: he shall smite and heal it: and they shall return even to the Lord, and he shall be intreated of them, and shall heal them. 23 In that day shall there be a highway out of Egypt to Assyria, and the Assyrian shall come into Egypt, and the Egyptian into Assyria, and the Egyptians shall serve with the Assyrians. 24 In that day shall Israel be the third with Egypt and with Assyria, even a blessing in the midst of the land:

Isaiah 19:18-24 KJV

The eighth & ninth prophecies seem to be a result of the fulfillment of the fifth prophecy, the Psalm 83 War. This segment of scripture predicts several things. It speaks of Egypt making a spiritual turn toward God, erecting altars to the Lord and making a vow to the Lord. It says the Egyptians shall know the Lord and shall do sacrifice to the Lord. It says that five cities in the land of Egypt shall speak the language of Canaan. These are all major events for an Arab county like Egypt, especially when we consider the quotes we looked at when we reviewed the first prophecy.

To help us better identify the fulfillment of this section of scripture, we are going to focus on two predictions that should be easily identifiable as the fulfillment of this prophecy. First, there shall be a highway built from Egypt to Assyria (northwestern Iraq) and second, there shall be some type of an alliance between Israel, Egypt and Assyria. Both of these prophecies are major and should be readily recognizable when they are fulfilled.

Summary

As we review these prophecies, not only did Israel become a new nation, but we have seen her enemies call for her destruction since the mid 1960s. We have seen Egypt go through the upheavals caused by the Muslim Brotherhood and a major dam is being built that could easily allow for the fourth prophecy to be fulfilled. The next three prophecies don't appear to have been fulfilled yet but the region is filled with so much turmoil that they could conceivably be fulfilled at any time in the near future. The last two prophecies appear to be a little further out on the horizon.

Chapter Three
Major End Time Prophecies

Prophecy	Description	Status
Initial	Israel a nation again	Fulfilled
1st	Thine enemies make a tumult	Fulfilled
2nd	Egyptian against Egyptian	Fulfilled
3rd	Egyptians given over to a cruel lord	Fulfilled
4th	The Nile river shall dry up	Strong potential for fulfillment
5th	Psalm 83 War	Partially fulfilled
6th	Damascus a ruinous heap	Unfulfilled
7th	Desolation of Moab and Ammon	Unfulfilled
8th & 9th	Five cities of Egypt speak Hebrew	Unfulfilled
	Highway from Egypt to Assyria	Unfulfilled

There is another major prophecy that we have not yet considered, that is Ezekiel's War as described in Ezekiel Chapters 38 and 39. We will look at it next, and by itself, since it deserves careful and special attention.

The Three Woes
A Guide To Understanding Revelation and End Time Prophecies

Worksheet Questions for Chapter 3

1. Can you quote someone who has made a statement fulfilling the Psalm 83:1-4 threat against Israel?

2. How long were the Muslim Brotherhood and the Egyptian authorities in an ongoing struggle for political control of Egypt?

3. In what year did the Muslim Brotherhood gain control of the Egyptian government?

4. What dam being built on the Blue Nile in Ethiopia has the potential of causing the Nile river in Egypt to dry up according to the scripture in Isaiah 19:5-6?

5. We looked at a total of ten prophecies in this chapter, how many of them have been fulfilled?

Chapter Four
Ezekiel's War

And the word of the Lord came unto me, saying, 2 Son of man, set thy face against Gog, the land of Magog, the chief prince of Meshech and Tubal, and prophesy against him, 3 And say, Thus saith the Lord God; Behold I am against thee, O Gog, the chief prince of Meshech and Tubal: 4 And I will turn thee back, and put hooks into thy jaws, and I will bring thee forth, and all thine army, horses and horsemen, all of them clothed with all sorts of armour, even a great company with bucklers and shields, all of them handling swords: 5 Persia, Ethiopia, and Libya with them; all of them with shield and helmet: 6 Gomer, and all his bands; the house of Togarmah of the north quarters, and all his bands: and many people with thee. 7 Be thou prepared, and prepare for thyself, thou, and all thy company that are assembled unto thee, and be thou a guard unto them. 8 After many days thou shalt be visited: in the latter years thou shalt come into the land that is brought back from the sword, and is gathered out of many people, against the mountains of Israel, which have been always waste: but it is brought forth out of the nations, and they shall dwell safely all of them. 9 Thou shalt ascend and come like a storm, thou shalt be like a cloud to cover the land, thou, and all thy bands, and many people with thee. 10 Thus saith the Lord God; It shall also come to pass, that at the same time shall things come into thy mind, and thou shalt think an evil thought: 11 And thou shalt say, I will go up to the land of unwalled villages; I will go to them that are at rest, that dwell safely, all of them dwelling without walls, and having neither bars nor gates, 12 To take a spoil, and to take a prey; to turn thine hand upon the desolate places that are now inhabited, and upon the people that are gathered out of the nations, which have gotten cattle and goods, that dwell in the midst of the land. 13 Sheba, and Dedan, and the merchants of Tarshish, with all the young lions thereof, shall say unto thee, Art

The Three Woes
A Guide To Understanding Revelation and End Time Prophecies

thou come to take a spoil? hast thou gathered thy company to take a prey? to carry away silver and gold, to take away cattle and goods, to take a great spoil? 14 Therefore, son of man, prophesy and say unto Gog, Thus saith the Lord God; In that day when my people of Israel dwelleth safely, shalt thou not know it? 15 And thou shalt come from thy place out of the north parts, thou, and many people with thee, all of them riding upon horses, a great company, and a mighty army: 16 And thou shalt come up against my people of Israel, as a cloud to cover the land; it shall be in the latter days, and I will bring thee against my land, that the heathen may know me, when I shall be sanctified in thee, O Gog, before their eyes. 17 Thus saith the Lord God; Art thou he of whom I have spoken in old time by my servants the prophets of Israel, which prophesied in those days many years that I would bring thee against them? 18 And it shall come to pass at the same time when Gog shall come against the land of Israel, saith the Lord God, that my fury shall come up in my face. 19 For in my jealousy and in the fire of my wrath have I spoken, Surely in that day there shall be a great shaking in the land of Israel; 20 So that the fishes of the sea, and the fowls of the heaven, and the beasts of the field, and all creeping things that creep upon the earth, and all the men that are upon the face of the earth, shall shake at my presence, and the mountains shall be thrown down, and the steep places shall fall, and every wall shall fall to the ground. 21 And I will call for a sword against him throughout all my mountains, saith the Lord God: every man's sword shall be against his brother. 22 And I will plead against him with pestilence and with blood; and I will rain upon him, and upon his bands, and upon the many people that are with him, an overflowing rain, and great hailstones, fire, and brimstone. 23 Thus will I magnify myself, and sanctify myself; and I will be known in the eyes of many nations, and they shall know that I am the Lord. 39:1 Therefore, thou son of man, prophesy against Gog, and say, Thus saith the Lord God; Behold, I am against thee, O Gog, the chief prince of Meshech and Tubal: 2 And

Chapter Four
Ezekiel's War

I will turn thee back, and leave but the sixth part of thee, and will cause thee to come up from the north parts, and will bring thee upon the mountains of Israel: 3 And I will smite thy bow out of thy left hand, and will cause thine arrows to fall out of thy right hand. 4 Thou shalt fall upon the mountains of Israel, thou, and all thy bands, and the people that is with thee: I will give thee unto the ravenous birds of every sort, and to the beasts of the field to be devoured. 5 Thou shalt fall upon the open field: for I have spoken it, saith the Lord God. 6 And I will send a fire on Magog, and among them that dwell carelessly in the isles: and they shall know that I am the Lord. 7 So will I make my holy name known in the midst of my people Israel; and I will not let them pollute my holy name any more: and the heathen shall know that I am the Lord, the Holy One in Israel. 8 Behold, it is come, and it is done, saith the Lord God; this is the day whereof I have spoken.
Ezekiel 38:1-39:8 KJV

This is a very lengthy section of scripture. Ezekiel's War, as it is called, actually covers three prophecies and runs from Ezekiel 38:1 through Ezekiel 39:16. The three prophecies are: the war, the burial of the dead, and the disposal of the weapons of war. For the purpose of this study we will only deal with the prophetic war, and not go into the burial of the dead and the cleanup of the weapons.

The Countries of Ezekiel's War

Modern Day Ezekiel's War Countries
Magog = **Russia**
Rosh = **Russia**
Gog = **Gogland is the Baltic Sea Region**
Meshech = **Black Sea Region**

Gomer = **Eastern Europe (Germany)**
Persia = **Iran**
Tubal = **Asia Minor**
Togarmah = **Southeastern Europe (Turkey)**
Ethiopia = **North Sudan**
Libya = **Libya**

The first thing we see in this prophecy is the list of countries that make up the coalition who have decided to attack Israel. We can see the interpretation of those historic names to their modern day regions and countries of the world in the chart above. The next thing that is seen is that Israel is living safely in unwalled villages. If you are a student of prophecy, you have probably noticed a lot in the news, on the internet, and on Christian programming about Ezekiel's War. It seems that, true Bible believers everywhere are straining their eyes and imaginations to will this prophecy into reality. Just because we don't see the fulfillment of it yet doesn't mean it won't come to pass. There are a number of issues with expecting the immediate fulfillment of this prophecy. Looking for the fulfillment of this prophecy in an untimely manner may cause us to miss other prophetic signs and warnings that are nearer at hand.

The Timing of Ezekiel's War

So, let's examine this prophecy in detail. We are told that Ezekiel's War will take place in the latter years. We all believe that we are living in the latter times, but even the disciples thought this. The point is, don't let the latter times be our only determining factor as to the time frame of the fulfillment of this prophecy. We are also told that Israel will be brought forth out of the nations, all of the people of Israel, and Israel will also be living safely, all of

Chapter Four
Ezekiel's War

Israel. This is certainly not the reality for Israel today, Israel is not a country living safely in unwalled villages.

Another issue of concern relative to this prophecy is the reference to Gog and Magog. When a Bible concordance search is performed for the phrase "Gog and Magog" and a search for "Gog" and also a search for "Magog", the only search results found are in Ezekiel Chapters 38 and 39 and in Revelation Chapter 20. What we must then ask ourselves is the following: Are these two references to Gog and Magog separate conflicts occurring a thousand years apart, or are they the same conflict? The reference to Gog and Magog in the Book of Revelation obviously occurs at the end of the 1,000 year Millennial reign of Christ. Is there also a Gog and Magog war that occurs before or during the Tribulation?

Ezekiel's Visions

To help us answer this question, we need to carefully study the Book of Ezekiel itself. As we read through the Book of Ezekiel, we find that Ezekiel defines thirteen specific times when he had a vision or Word from God. Between these specific occurrences, Ezekiel would frequently say that he further heard from the Lord, or that the Word of the Lord came to him, or the hand of the Lord was upon him, etc. We must now question if these are separate visions? Are they completely separate and unrelated visions, or are they a continuation of the original dated vision? Could they be dealing with the same subject but only from a slightly modified view point? Are they just an ongoing conversation between Ezekiel and the Lord all within the same vision?

The Three Woes
A Guide To Understanding Revelation and End Time Prophecies

	Ezekiel's Visions		
	Scripture Reference	Reference Date	Manner of Vision
1	Ezekiel 1:1	Year 13, Month 4, Day 5	I saw visions of God
2	Ezekiel 8:1	Year 6, Month 6, Day 5	the hand of God fell on me
3	Ezekiel. 20:1	Year 7, Month 5, Day 10	the Word of the Lord came to me
4	Ezekiel 24:1	Year 9, Month 10, Day 10	the Word of the Lord came to me
5	Ezekiel 26:1	Year 11, Day 1	the Word of the Lord came to me
6	Ezekiel 29:1	Year 10, Month 10, Day 12	the Word of the Lord came to me
7	Ezekiel 29:17	Year 27, Month 1, Day 1	the Word of the Lord came to me
8	Ezekiel 30:20	Year 11, Month 1, Day 7	the Word of the Lord came to me
9	Ezekiel 31:1	Year 11, Month 3, Day 1	the Word of the Lord came to me
10	Ezekiel 32:1	Year 12, Month 12, Day 1	the Word of the Lord came to me
11	Ezekiel 32:17	Year 12 Month 12, Day 15	the Word of the Lord came to me
12	Ezekiel 33:21	Year 12, Month 10, Day 5	the Word of the Lord came to me
13	Ezekiel 40:1	Year 25, Month 1, Day 10	the hand of the Lord was on me

Let's assume for the moment that Ezekiel only had thirteen visions and that each of those visions occurred on a specific date as defined by Ezekiel and shown in the chart above. Let us also assume that when Ezekiel stated that he further heard from the

Chapter Four
Ezekiel's War

Lord, that it was a continuation of the dated vision and not a new and separate vision.

Based on the above assumptions, the specific vision that contains the prophecy against Gog and Magog is found at Ezekiel 33:21. So, let's examine this vision along with its seven sub-visions. The initial vision within this prophesy is a prophetic curse against the inhabitants of the wasted promise land that was Israel. The second part of this vision was a prophetic curse against the shepherds of Israel who failed to rightly lead the flock of Israel while they were in the Promised Land. The prophecy went on to say that the people of Israel would someday be restored to the Promised Land and that my servant David shall be their shepherd.

	Sub-Vision	Sub-Vision Description
1	Ezekiel 33:21	The enemy inhabitants of Israel
2	Ezekiel 34:1	Woe to the shepherds of Israel and the restoration of Israel to the land
3	Ezekiel 35:1	Set thy face against mount Seir
4	Ezekiel 36:1	Prophesy to the mountains of Israel
5	Ezekiel 36:16	Prophesy to the house of Israel
6	Ezekiel 37:1	Prophesy to the dry bones
7	Ezekiel 37:15	The unity of Israel (Judah and Israel one)
8	Ezekiel 38:1	Prophesy to Gog and Magog

> *And I will set up one shepherd over them, and he shall feed them, even my servant David; he shall feed them, and he shall be their shepherd.*
> **Ezekiel 34:23 KJV**

The third part of this vision is a prophetic curse against the people and land of mount Seir (modern day Jordan) because of their hatred toward the Israeli people of the Promised Land. The fourth part of this vision is to the mountains of Israel (the Promised Land) that they shall shoot forth and yield fruit.

> *And I will multiply upon you man and beast; and they shall increase and bring fruit: and I will settle you after your old estates, and will do better unto you than at your beginnings: and ye shall know that I am the Lord.*
> **Ezekiel 36:11 KJV**

The fifth part of this vision is a prophecy to the house of Israel. Part of the people of Israel shall return to the Promised Land and the land will blossom like the Garden of Eden. Notice, however, that the people will be living in fenced and fortified cities. This is a pretty accurate picture of present day Israel.

> *And they shall say, This land that was desolate is become like the garden of Eden; and the waste and desolate and ruined cities are become fenced, and are inhabited.*
> **Ezekiel 36:35 KJV**

The sixth part of the vision is a prophesy of the dry bones. The whole of Israel will be restored to the promised land of Israel. The whole house of Israel means all of Judah and all of the lost tribes of Israel.

> *Then he said unto me, Son of man, these bones are the whole house of Israel: ...*
> **Ezekiel 37:11 KJV**

The seventh part of the vision is a prophecy of the coming unity of the house of Israel. Not only will Judah and the house of Israel be restored to the Promised Land, but they will be united and living under the rule of King David (Jesus). They will also enjoy an everlasting covenant of peace for evermore. This is certainly not a picture of Israel today.

> *And David my servant shall be king over them; and they all shall have one shepherd: they shall also walk in my judgments, and observe my statutes, and do them. 25 And they shall dwell in the land that I have given unto Jacob my servant, wherein your fathers have dwelt; and they shall dwell therein, even they, and their children, and their children's children for ever: and my servant David shall be their prince for ever. 26 Moreover I will make a covenant of peace with them; it shall be an everlasting covenant with them: and I will place them, and multiply them, and will set my sanctuary in the midst of them for evermore.*
> **Ezekiel 37:24-26 KJV**

Review of Ezekiel's Vision

Let's review this Ezekiel 33:21 vision along with its eight individual sub-visions, that was experienced by Ezekiel in the twelfth year, tenth month and fifth day of his captivity. As we look over these seven sub-visions leading up to the eighth sub-vision being the prophecy of Gog and Magog, it is easy to see the continuity of these visions. Ezekiel is seeing God's prophetic vision for the promise land, his chosen people and their enemies from the time of their exile to the time of their return to their land in 1948 and on to the reign of Jesus during the Millennium. Our generation of today has had the opportunity to see the fulfillment of the first five of these sub-visions. The Promised Land is currently occupied by some of the Jewish people and the land is blossoming like the Garden of Eden for them. What has not yet come to pass is the fulfillment of the last three of these sub-visions. The three that are yet to be fulfilled are the return of the rest of Israel to the

Promised Land, the uniting of Judah with the rest of Israel under the reign of Christ and then the Battle of Gog and Magog.

Even if you don't want to accept that this prophecy in Ezekiel 33:21 is one ongoing prophecy with eight sub-prophecies and decide to believe that the Gog and Magog prophecy of Ezekiel 38:1 is a standalone prophecy, there is still another major hurdle to overcome for it to be fulfilled today. Ezekiel 38:11 and Ezekiel 39:26 describe what life is like in Israel (the Promised Land) at the time of Ezekiel's war.

> And thou shalt say, I will go up to the land of unwalled villages; I will go to them that are at rest, that dwell safely, all of them dwelling without walls, and having neither bars nor gates,
> **Ezekiel 38:11 KJV**

> Therefore thus saith the Lord God; Now will I bring again the captivity of Jacob, and have mercy upon the whole house of Israel, and will be jealous for my holy name;
> **Ezekiel 39:25 KJV**

> After that they have borne their shame, and all their trespasses whereby they have trespassed against me, when they dwelt safely in their land, and none made them afraid.
> **Ezekiel 39:26 KJV**

Israel Today

What we see in these verses doesn't sound like the Israel of today. Israel currently has several hundred miles of fortified walls around the country. In the past they have installed an Arrow Missile Interceptor system, David's Sling, sometimes called Magic

Chapter Four
Ezekiel's War

Wand, and Israel currently has a missile defense system called the Iron Dome. They have over a million bomb shelters in the country and since 1951, every home, business and building has been required to have access to a bomb shelter. Some regions of the country have fortified bus stops and over the years the government has issued several million gas masks.

These three verses above are specifically describing the time of Ezekiel's war. No walls, no bars, no gates, dwelling safely and unafraid. If you are dwelling safely and unafraid, then you certainly don't need Iron Dome Missile Defense systems and bomb shelters.

Description of Ezekiel's War

As we look further at the eighth sub-vision of Gog and Magog, the prophecy provides us with an insight into the manner in which this war will be won. Most wars are won because of either: a stronger force, a strategic or economic advantage, or some other human based power that ultimately produces victory for one side or the other. But in Ezekiel's War, God declares that His fury rises up in His face and He, God, fights against the enemies of Israel. God says He will use a great shaking in the land of Israel, an earthquake in modern day terms. Let's take a look at what impact an extremely forceful and wide spread earthquake might have on an attacking force. First of all, let's keep in mind that the attacking force would be made up of an army that speaks at least five or six different languages, Russian, German, Turkish, Arabic, English, Libyan and Persian. Second, most major modern battles or initial attacks are initiated after the sun has gone down so the cover of darkness can offer an advantage. Now picture again a major wide spread earthquake taking place during a major battle or a surprise attack during the dark of night and the attacking forces speaking as many as five or six different languages. How much confusion and disarray might such circumstances cause an attacking force? God says every man's sword will be against his brothers. How easy is it to picture enough confusion and chaos that there would be a great loss of life due to what we would call "friendly fire?"

In addition to the friendly fire, that is likely to erupt, God says that He will also send an overflowing rain, and great hailstones, fire and brimstone. The overflowing rain and earthquake would probably mean that many bridges are damaged and out of service and the rivers would become impassable barriers. Great hailstones, just how great is this? Most of us have seen small marble sized hailstones and we've seen photos of golf ball and baseball sized hailstones and the damage they have left. But who has seen great hailstones? In Revelation 16:21 we are told that there will be hail that will weigh a talent. According to history, a common talent weighed 75 pounds and a royal talent weighed 150 pounds. A 35 pound block of ice (29" x 14" x 5 1/2") is about the size of four shoeboxes. The damage that would be caused by ice of this size and weight is nearly unimaginable.

The end result of Ezekiel's War is that only one sixth of the army that goes against Israel will survive. That means that 83% of the coalition forces sent against Israel will be slain. That is an amazing and an over whelming defeat any way you look at it.

What we have just seen described is God fighting a war against Israel's enemies. It is interesting to note God's covenant of peace with Israel in Ezekiel 37:26, just two verses before the vision of the Gog and Magog battle where God fights the battle for Israel because of the covenant He made with Israel.

The main take away from this study in Ezekiel is to know just where we are in God's timeline of the ages. Don't be deceived as

Chapter Four
Ezekiel's War

to how late the hour is because you are looking for the fulfillment of a prophecy a thousand years ahead of time.

In the next chapter we will look at several less significant yet highly recognizable prophecies that can help to pin point where we are in God's timeline.

The Three Woes
A Guide To Understanding Revelation and End Time Prophecies

Worksheet Questions for Chapter 4

1. How many specific prophecies can be found in Ezekiel 38:1 - 39:8 and what are they?

2. What are the two prevalent descriptions for Israel at the time of Ezekiel's War?

3. Where in the Bible can we find references to Gog and Magog?

4. How many times did Ezekiel provide a specific date of when he had a vision from the Lord and where in Ezekiel are they located?

5. If we examine Ezekiel's ninth vision found in Ezekiel 33:21, how many sub-visions does this vision have and what are they?

Chapter Four
Ezekiel's War

6. What are the last three sub-visions of Ezekiel 33:21 that are yet to be fulfilled?

7. How many pounds will the great hailstones of Revelation 16:21 weigh?

8. How large is a 35 pound block of ice?

The Three Woes
A Guide To Understanding Revelation and End Time Prophecies

Chapter Five
Are We Living in the End Times?

The Olivet Discourse

One of the first scriptures we should examine to see if we are living in the end times is Matthew Chapter 24. It is in Matthew along with Mark Chapter 13 and Luke Chapter 21 that we find Jesus' Olivet Discourse. For this discussion, we will limit our scope of investigation to Matthew's version of the discourse. Jesus' disciples ask Him three specific questions. The first question is, "When shall these things be?" where His disciples are referring to the destruction of the temple buildings. The second and third questions are, "What shall be the sign of thy coming, and the end of the world?"

What we have here are three distinct questions, but depending on your point of view there may be multiple answers to those questions or no answer at all. The first question as to the destruction of the temple may or may not have been answered; it's hard to say being nearly two thousand years removed from that event. It seems that the discourse can be divided into five components. The components of most interest to us are the first three.

THE COMPONENTS OF THE OLIVET DISCOURSE	
Matt. 24: 4-14	A description of the worsening conditions in the world leading up to the rapture of the church.
Matt. 24:15-22	A description of a major even that will usher in the second half of the tribulation and the end of the world (the Wrath of God) as we know it.

The Three Woes
A Guide To Understanding Revelation and End Time Prophecies

Matt. 24:23-31	A description of the rapture of the church and a description of the signs to look for just before its occurrence.
Matt. 24:32 - Matt. 25:30	A description via parables of the time just prior to the rapture of the church and how the church should watch and live to be prepared for Christ's coming.
Matt. 25:31-46	A picture of the Millennial Age and the end time judgments.

If the question as to when the temple buildings would be destroyed is answered, it would have been answered somewhere between Verses 4 and 14 of Matthew Chapter 24. Whether it was or was not answered is somewhat immaterial to us. What is of most importance to us is that these verses certainly apply to the time since the disciples asked the question and to our time today. There are a lot of things mentioned that we should be looking for, rumors of wars, wars, pestilences, earthquakes, afflictions, betrayals, but the most significant and often repeated sign to look for is that of deception. If you are sufficiently deceived, all the other signs could be present, yet they could be overlooked or ignored.

In the following paragraphs I will be dealing with some subject matter that could be construed by some as controversial or hateful. There is no intention whatsoever to disparage or in any way hurt any individual or group of individuals. They, just like everyone else have been given, by God, their free will to live as they please. However, I will not apologize for my beliefs and view points on such matters, nor for God's Word on such matters.

Chapter Five
Are We Living in the End Times?

Deception

And Jesus answered and said unto them, Take heed that no man deceive you.
Matthew 24:4 KJV

For many shall come in my name, saying, I am Christ; and shall deceive many.
Matthew 24:5 KJV

And many false prophets shall rise, and shall deceive many.
Matthew 24:11 KJV

For there shall arise false Christs, and false prophets, and shall shew great signs and wonders; insomuch that, if it were possible, they shall deceive the very elect.
Matthew 24:24 KJV

Throughout time man has chosen to do that which God has declared man should not do. It began when the serpent beguiled Eve and she ate from the tree that was forbidden. God had told Adam and Eve that they would die if they ate of the tree of the knowledge of good and evil. But Eve was deceived by the serpent and she ate, and Adam ate of it also. Since the beginning of time man has been vulnerable to deception.

Does anyone see any signs of deception in our time? Jesus says that this is what we should guard ourselves against. Depending on what news media you tune into, the views of the world are as different as night and day. It seems that some news media present the world from a liberal point of view while some other news media present the world from a conservative point of view.

The Three Woes
A Guide To Understanding Revelation and End Time Prophecies

The liberal point of view tells us that global warming, now called climate change, will cause the world to come to an end in just a few short years. The conservative view rejects the global warming hypothesis. Many experts attempt to offer proof against global warming only to have their arguments dismissed and their names disparaged. Even in this we can see deceit and hypocrisy.

So, who should we believe the liberals or the conservatives? In Genesis 8:22 God tells us *"While the earth remaineth, seedtime and harvest, cold and heat, and summer and winter, and day and night shall not cease."* Whom shall we believe, God or man? How ironic that the world tells us that climate change is going to destroy the world, yet God tells us in Revelation how He will destroy the earth one day and the world chooses to scoff.

We are living in an age where men claim to be women and women claim to be men. We are living in a time when parents and schools are pushing children to claim to be a sex that is different than when they were born. California and other states are now offering non-binary options in place of male and female for birth certificate designations. Yet if you choose to disapprove of this progressive or liberal life style in any way, you are labeled a bigot, a purveyor of hate speech, and in some places you may be charged with a crime. Yet God said in Genesis 1:27 *"So God created man in his own image, in the image of God created he him; male and female created he them."*

Throughout history there have been occurrences of same sex relationships. Though they existed, they usually were kept private and the general population was mostly unaware of them. Over the past few decades however, there has been a marked change. Not only has the LGBTQ community come out of the closet as they call it, but it seems as if they wish to make their lifestyle part of mainstream society. Everywhere we turn; the lifestyle is being

Chapter Five
Are We Living in the End Times?

pushed as the norm even though it is only about 4.5% of the United States population according to a 2017 Gallup poll. We see it in major box office movies, we see it in television programs, we see it promoted in commercial programming on television. We have seen lawsuits arise where individuals and small businesses have been sued because they have chosen to not perform a service or function that would cause them to violate their Christian beliefs. All too frequently, it can even be seen as a major dividing factor within many church denominations as well as local congregations.

> *Professing themselves to be wise, they became fools, 23 And changed the glory of the uncorruptible God into an image made like to corruptible man, and to birds, and fourfooted beasts, and creeping things. 24 Wherefore God also gave them up to uncleanness through the lusts of their own hearts, to dishonour their own bodies between themselves: 25 Who changed the truth of God into a lie, and worshipped and served the creature more than the Creator, who is blessed for ever. Amen. 26 For this cause God gave them up unto vile affections: for even their women did change the natural use into that which is against nature: 27 And likewise also the men, leaving the natural use of the woman, burned in their lust one toward another; men with men working that which is unseemly, and receiving in themselves that recompence of their error which was meet. 28 And even as they did not like to retain God in their knowledge, God gave them over to a reprobate mind, to do those things which are not convenient; 29 Being filled with all unrighteousness, fornication, wickedness, covetousness, maliciousness; full of envy, murder, debate, deceit, malignity; whisperers,*
> **Romans 1:22-29 KJV**

The Three Woes
A Guide To Understanding Revelation and End Time Prophecies

One of the greatest deceptions of our age is that of Roe vs. Wade and the issue of abortion. Since the landmark case of Roe vs. Wade in 1973, there have been over sixty million innocent children murdered in the United States. But this is not an issue affecting just the United States, it is a worldwide problem. Around the world young women, mothers, have been convinced that it is their right to have control over their bodies, their right to choose whether to have a pregnancy, or not to have a pregnancy.

That right to choose is theirs, but they made that choice when they chose to get pregnant. They had every right to take actions to prevent a pregnancy. They had every right to abstain from having sex, but they have no moral right to take the life of an innocent and helpless unborn child just because they made a prior bad choice. The world doesn't teach them to be moral, responsible, mature adults that accept the consequences of their decisions and actions. Because of the deception of abortion, there are now millions of women who find themselves, later in life, suffering the guilt and shame of having murdered their own child.

Many of the same individuals, who so freely promote and exalt the virtues of abortion, are at the same time staunch supporters of PETA and ASPCA. PETA, People for the Ethical Treatment of Animals, and ASPCA, American Society for the Prevention of Cruelty to Animals, are both American organizations working to stop animal abuse and fighting to prevent animal cruelty. Animals certainly shouldn't be treated cruelly or in an abusive manner. But, the irony is, that many PETA and ASPCA supporters openly advocate for the abortion of innocent unborn children. Anyone who thinks that abortion isn't cruel or abusive should watch the movies "*Unplanned*" and "*Gosnell: The Trial of America's Biggest Serial Killer.*"

Chapter Five
Are We Living in the End Times?

Does anyone see deceit and apostasy at work in our world today?

Next, we will briefly cover the other signs from Matthew Chapter 24 that Jesus told us we should be watching for. The signs that we should be looking for in the end times were "rumors of wars, wars, pestilences, earthquakes, afflictions and betrayals."

Rumors of Wars and Wars

Let's start by examining the issue of rumors of war and wars. If one does an Internet Google search on the term "history of war" you can see the following statement, "**War** is defined as an active conflict that has claimed more than 1,000 lives. Of the past 3,400 years, humans have been entirely at peace for only 268 of them, or just 8 percent of recorded history."

In just the past 125 years mankind has witnessed two world wars and concern over the potential of a third world war has been constantly with us ever since the Cuban missile crisis of the 1960s. The first world war saw approximately 20 million people killed and the Second World War saw the loss of life accelerate to an estimated 70 to 85 million individuals. Since the introduction of nuclear weapons at the conclusion of world War Two, the world has seen the size and power of those weapons increase by more than a hundred fold. These weapons have proliferated to the point where multiple countries have tens of thousands of them. These nuclear weapons, along with other radiological, chemical and biological weapons, have come to be known as weapons of mass destruction because of the over whelming damage they are capable of producing. For at least the past fifty years, there have been talks and rumors of man totally destroying himself and the earth, as mankind continually lives on the brink of a potential third world war. It is rumored that if a third world war occurred, the casualties would number into the billions. Does this describe the end time that Jesus forewarned us about?

Pestilences

Pestilences were the next items we were told to watch for in the end times. Since the beginning of the Twentieth Century we have seen many pestilences affect different regions of the world and a few have impacted the entire world. One of the most notable and deadly of these was the 1918 flu pandemic that was estimated to have taken the lives of up to 100 million people. Another major example was the worldwide HIV/AIDS pandemic that began in the second half of the Twentieth Century and continues on today. It seems to be less of a pandemic now than it was, but since its emergence, it has taken approximately 30 million lives.

Earthquakes

The next item in the list that Jesus gave us to watch for is earthquakes in diverse places.

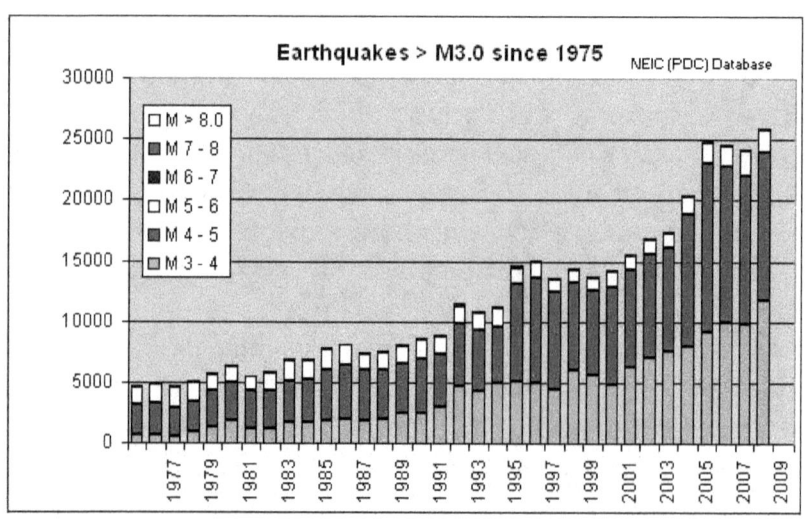

Chapter Five
Are We Living in the End Times?

This graph from the National Earthquake Information Center (*NEIC*), a division of the US Geological Survey, a scientific agency of the US government, shows a dramatic increase in earthquakes just since 1977. The number of magnitude three through five earthquakes has been increasing dramatically since the end of the last century.

Afflictions

The definition of an affliction is a curse to bear, or something that causes agony, suffering, or great pain. Polio was a prominent disease during the 1950s that caused wide spread affliction. Fortunately, a vaccine was created in the 1950s and the disease has been nearly eradicated. Cancer is another affliction that has brought wide spread affliction and distress to many around the world. Although modern medicine has made great strides in its fight against this disease, cancer still remains one of the most dreaded words in our language due to the extreme suffering and pain that we all associate with it. Autism and Alzheimer's are other afflictions that we see so prevalent in our time.

Betrayals

Last in the list of the signs that we were told to watch for by Jesus was betrayals. So where might we find evidence of betrayal? Many countries around the world have made it so difficult to be a Christian that many believers must gather and worship in secret. To do otherwise, they risk imprisonment or potential death. In America, we have been blessed, that this is not the case here. Due to the freedoms established by our founding fathers we are able to worship and believe as we wish.

But, there are other forms of betrayal besides just physical betrayal. If we look in the right areas, we can see examples of betrayal in our society as well. The betrayal in our society comes via the sign we were most warned about, deceit. Let's look at a couple of examples. Walt Disney is a household name in our society and around the world. The company he formed became famous around the world for the wholesome, family and child oriented quality entertainment that it produced for many decades. However, Disney has been pressured by the LGBTQ community to portray more openly gay relationships in their shows and movies. In an episode of the XD Series "Star vs. the Forces of Evil" that aired recently, Disney showed several gay kisses. This is not the kind of programming young children should be subjected to. Another case in point is the TV series "The Owl House." Life Site News says, "Disney introduces kids to a world of demons and witchcraft in the new 'The Owl House' show." This is betrayal to the extreme. A company that the world has come to love and trust, we must now censor, and worry about what subtle message may be getting promoted to our very young children.

But it is not just the youngest children that are in danger. We see the same happening with our young adult children as well. America is filled with centers for higher learning. Many of the original centers of higher education were founded with the specific purpose of training ministers of the Gospel of Jesus Christ and promoting Christian values and Christian thought. Yet today most of Americas' centers of higher education have become centers of liberal thought and liberal ideas, where conservative ideas and Christian values are unwelcome. Indeed, the colleges and universities have become safe zones, where those conservative ideas and Christian values are not allowed to be discussed or even presented for consideration. Many parents send their young adult children to these schools unaware of what they are really being taught.

Chapter Five
Are We Living in the End Times?

College	Founding	Founding Purpose
Harvard University	1636	Originally called "New College", its purpose was mainly to educate clergy. It was renamed Harvard University in 1639 after the Rev. John Harvard.
College of William and Mary	1693	King William III and Queen Mary II of England signed the charter for a "perpetual College of Divinity, Philosophy, Languages, and other good Arts and Sciences" in 1693.
Yale University	1701	Yale Chartered by Connecticut Colony, the "Collegiate School" was established in 1701 by clergy to educate Congregational ministers.
Princeton University	1746	New Light Presbyterians founded the College of New Jersey, later Princeton University, in 1746 in order to train ministers dedicated to their views.
Dartmouth College	1769	Dartmouth College was founded in 1769 by Eleazar Wheelock, a Congregational minister from Columbia, Connecticut, who had sought to establish a school to train Native Americans as Christian missionaries.

The Three Woes
A Guide To Understanding Revelation and End Time Prophecies

Now that we have covered the signs that Jesus warned us to watch for, we can ask, are there any other signs that might offer additional clues as to how near the return of Jesus really is?

Forbidding To Marry

Forbidding to marry, and commanding to abstain from meats, which God hath created to be received with thanksgiving of them which believe and know the truth.
1 Timothy 4:3 KJV

Another end time prophecy is found in the verse above. We know that this is an end time prophecy because in 1 Timothy 4:1 it says "*Now..., in the latter times*". The main point for us to look at in this verse is the phrase "abstain from meats." As the global warming crowd expounds their philosophy, they have focused in on CO_2 emissions. Their argument is that mankind's only way to stop global warming is to lower CO_2 emissions. Their argument comes up lacking, in that mans' CO_2 emissions per year amount to less CO_2 than is produced by just one volcanic eruption. If mankind was able to eliminate all manmade CO_2 emissions, it would lower total CO_2 emissions less than one percent. The true reason for pushing the lowering of CO_2 emissions is to promote the redistribution of wealth. The major emphasis is to bolster fear and thereby to get wealthy industrialized countries to buy carbon credits from non-industrialized poor countries. The buying of the carbon credits does nothing to change the CO_2 emission rate of mankind; its only impact is to transfer wealth from a rich country to a poor country. Out of this CO_2 charade has arisen an argument against eating meat and eliminating the beef industry, because cows produce methane gas as part of their life process.

Chapter Five
Are We Living in the End Times?

Calling Evil Good, and Good Evil

Woe unto them that call evil good, and good evil; that put darkness for light, and light for darkness; that put bitter for sweet, and sweet for bitter!
Isaiah 5:20 KJV

We spoke earlier about the view of the world differing according to the perspective of the news program that one might choose to listen to, or how your world view differs depending on whether you look at the world from a liberal point of view or from a conservative point of view. There is no question that we are living in a highly divided world. In the verse above, although it is not a specific end time prophecy, it does paint a very accurate description of our world today. It is a warning for every age to not call evil good or to call good evil.

It is a very fascinating verse to consider. In the past few years, there have been examples of both of the above mentioned world views using this verse to drive home their message and to confirm that their world view is not only the correct view, but that it also aligns with God's view.

Take heed therefore that the light which is in thee be not darkness.
Luke 11:35

Liberal View Point Example Argument
Conservative Christians condemn homosexuals and their lifestyle. They discriminate against them and claim that God has not forgiven them. How can they be so unforgiving and hateful when God says He loves everyone? Racism, bigotry, xenophobia and sexism are their' so called Christian values. They call evil good and good evil.

Conservative View Point Example Argument
Liberal Christians welcome homosexuals and their lifestyle. They embrace them within the body of the church and even welcome them as Pastors and church leaders. How can they ignore God's condemnation against this perverted lifestyle. Why do they think my moral values are hate speech? They call evil good and good evil.

So what is going on here? Can both of these viewpoints be true? Can they both possibly line up with God's Word? No way! One of these two arguments has been caught in the middle of great deception. That was the major warning sign from Jesus. So what do we do? How do we determine which viewpoint aligns with God? Prayer and the study of God's Word is the only way to discern the truth. The following prayer would be a good starting place for anyone with a desire to know the truth.

> Almighty God, whatever I'm calling good in my life that is evil, or evil in my life that is good – all according to Your standards, please, make me aware and help me change. Amen.

The next thing we should do is evaluate what we believe and then study God's Word. Do our beliefs align with God's Word? Are the words we are using to characterize our beliefs accurate or deceptive? Semantics are very important. As we saw earlier in our discussion, global warming is now called climate change. Did the definition change when the name changed? Not at all! But the believability and the ability to deceive, definitely increased. Who wouldn't believe in climate change? We see the seasons change every few months and the weather changes weekly if not daily.

Chapter Five
Are We Living in the End Times?

Semantics are very important. We can use semantics to turn our morals into acceptance. A little hocus-pocus and all of sudden evil is good and good is evil. Take an example of pornography. Call it art and it's no longer evil. Really? He called it consensual sex. She called it rape. Which was it? We are living in an age where man has mastered the art of calling things by new names that successfully alter their real character or meaning. Man is carefully polishing off every edge and point and corner that might prick conscience into activity. We are toning down our moral values until we can hardly tell for certain what is right and what is wrong, what is evil and what is good.

The simple truth is that preachers are not preaching the simple truth. As preaching has drifted further and further from the Bible, so the people who hear such preaching have drifted further and further from the Bible and God's truth. The only solution is to go back to the Bible as the final and absolute revelation of God's will and as the final standard of what is right and what is wrong.

So, let's return to our example of the liberal and conservative viewpoints. The liberal says, God is love and how can the conservative be so hateful. The conservative says, God condemned the homosexual lifestyle and how can the liberal accept it.

Billy Graham says the following:

"Modern man does not like to think of God in terms of wrath, anger and judgment. He likes to make God according to his own ideas and give God the characteristics he wants Him to possess. Man tries to remake God to conform to his own wishful thinking, so that he can make himself comfortable in his sins.

> This modern god has the attributes of love, mercy and forgiveness, but is without justice. Man doesn't want to be judged and punished for sin. He "reconstructs" God along the lines of tolerance, all-embracing love and universal goodwill."

The truth is, God is love. He loved the homosexual, the conservative and the liberal so much that He gave His Son's life for their sins. But that love from God must be accepted by the sinner and that sinner must repent and turn from his sin. God is also just. God clearly says in His Word that those who are sinners shall not inherit the kingdom of God. God is truth and God can not lie.

> *For God so loved the world, that he gave his only begotten Son, that whosoever believeth in him should not perish, but have everlasting life.*
> **John 3:16 KJV**

> *Know ye not that the unrighteous shall not inherit the kingdom of God? Be not deceived: neither fornicators, nor idolaters, nor adulterers, nor effeminate, nor abusers of themselves with mankind, 10 Nor thieves, nor covetous, nor drunkards, nor revilers, nor extortioners, shall inherit the kingdom of God.*
> **1 Corinthians 6:9-10 KJV**

We have just reviewed a lengthy list of scriptures to determine if the days that we are living in are in fact the last days just prior to the return of Jesus Christ. No one can say with absolute certainty, but our days definitely seem to fit the description of the last days. Have we exhausted all the scripture texts that we could look at? No, not at all. From prophetic scripture we know a third temple will exist during the tribulation and throughout Israel there is talk of rebuilding the temple. Most if not all of the temple vessels have

Chapter Five
Are We Living in the End Times?

been replaced and are ready for service. Much is being discussed concerning the "Abraham Accords", the proposed peace plan between Israel and her neighbors. Could this plan be the one that will usher in the tribulation period? Only time will tell.

In the next chapter, we will look at the Book of Revelation itself to see if we can unravel some of the mysteries and symbolisms that have made the Book of Revelation so confusing and difficult to understand for so many.

The Three Woes
A Guide To Understanding Revelation and End Time Prophecies

Worksheet Questions for Chapter 5

1. What are the five components of the Olivet Discourse in Matthew Chapters 24 and 25?

2. What is the most significant and often repeated sign in the Olivet Discourse that Jesus tells us to watch for?

3. What can we learn from Genesis 8:22?

4. In the Olivet Discourse, what four other signs besides deceit, did Jesus tell us to watch for?

5. What are two ways in which people in America are being betrayed?

Chapter Six
Understanding Revelation's Mysteries

As we said earlier, some written imagery and visual symbols found in the Book of Revelation will likely remain mysteries to us until we actually see the answer to the mystery unfold before us and the prophetic vision plays itself out. But, it also seems that we are living so close to the final moments before the return of Jesus to catch away his church and faithful followers, that we should be able to develop some educated theories and hypotheses about what John is describing. Indeed, that is why God gave us the Book of Revelation along with the other prophetic warnings. God does not want any of us to be caught unaware.

> *We have also a more sure word of prophecy; whereunto ye do well that ye take heed, as unto a light that shineth in a dark place, until the day dawn, and the day star arise in your hearts:*
> **2 Peter 1:19 KJV**

The first mystery that we are going to look at in the Book of Revelation is the mystery of the seven churches. Some claim that these are just salutations to seven individual churches that existed in Asia Minor at the time that the apostle John wrote the Book of Revelation. There are others who believe that these churches represent both the seven churches in Asia Minor but are also representative of seven unique time frames within the church age. Under this theory, each unique time span represents a sequential frame of time beginning at the time of the apostle John through to the rapture of the church and the end of the church age.

The Three Woes
A Guide To Understanding Revelation and End Time Prophecies

Christ writes seven epistles, one to each of seven churches in Asia Minor and each epistle follows the same template. As you read Jesus' critique of each church assembly, keep in mind that the word "angel" is likely referring to the pastor or overseer of that particular church. Also, know that these seven individual letters (four in chapter 2 and three in chapter 3 are all from Jesus Christ and not from John. John is merely the recorder of the message. Therefore, the first thing we see in each letter is what could easily be mistaken for a salutation to the pastor but is really more like a mailing address. After this address we find the command instructing John to write. We have now reached the beginning of the message that Jesus has for this particular pastor and congregation.

Now that we have reached the heart of the message, the first thing Jesus does is to proclaim who He is. In each letter, Jesus selects some personal attribute pertaining to His Deity and Authority over the pastor and the congregation that He is about to critique. Jesus then states that He knows the churches' works and He proceeds to review both the good and the bad that He sees within the church body. Jesus closes with a recommendation of how to be a more faithful and obedient servant and issues a promise of eternal blessing to all those who are willing to be over comers.

Once again we see Jesus declaring His Deity and authority through the promise He makes to each individual church pastor and congregation. This is a promise that only Jesus, being the Son of God, can make and keep. Every over comer will be the beneficiary of the promises made to each church.

Chapter Six
Understanding Revelation's Mysteries

The First Four Seals - The Four Horsemen of the Apocalypse

This section of scripture is one of the most misunderstood and misinterpreted prophetic passages in the Bible. For years, scholars have focused on the color of the horses instead of focusing on the activities of the riders. Because the first horse is white, many assume that the rider is Jesus and many others assume the rider is the antichrist because the rider is going off conquering and to conquer. In fact, the rider is neither. We don't see scholars assigning specific individuals to the riders of the red, pale or black horses and neither should they do so to the white horse.

The key to understanding the activities of the riders of each of these horses is found in Jesus' Olivet discourse in Matthew 24:4-7. There is a direct parallel between what Jesus told His disciples to look for in the end times prior to His coming and what we see occurring with the opening of the seals in Revelation Chapter 6. Jesus calls out five things to watch for in the end times and these five characteristic events of the end time match the first five seals of Revelation Chapter 6. These events are listed in the table below.

Warning	Event	Revelation Seal	Revelation Horse
Watch For 1	Deception	First Seal	White Horse
Watch For 2	Wars	Second Seal	Red Horse
Watch For 3	Famines	Third Seal	Black Horse
Watch For 4	Pestilences	Fourth Seal	Pale Horse
Watch For 5	Persecution	Fifth Seal	

In the next table we can see the parallels between the Revelation seals and the Matthew warnings. You might say the first seal doesn't match, but it does. We generally associate the color white as good and decent and the color black as bad or evil. In this case, we see a white horse, or good horse, but he is going forth to conquer. This horse is trying to hide its true intent. It is attempting to deceive.

	REVELATION SEALS	MATTHEW PARALLEL
S E A L 1 S E A L 1	And I saw when the Lamb opened one of the seals, and I heard, as it were the noise of thunder, one of the four beasts saying, Come and see. And I saw, and behold a white horse: and he that sat on him had a bow; and a crown was given unto him: and he went forth conquering, and to conquer. Revelation 6:1-2 KJV	And Jesus answered and said unto them, Take heed that no man deceive you. For many shall come in my name, saying, I am Christ; and shall deceive many. Matthew 24:4-5 KJV
S E A L 2	And when he had opened the second seal, I heard the second beast say, Come and see. And there went out another horse that was red: and power was given to him that sat thereon to take peace from the earth, and that they should kill one another: and there was given unto him a great sword. Revelation 6:3-4 KJV	And ye shall hear of wars and rumours of wars: see that ye be not troubled: for all these things must come to pass, but the end is not yet. For nation shall rise against nation, and kingdom against kingdom... Matthew 24:6-7a KJV
	And when he had opened the third seal, I heard the third beast say, Come and	...and there shall be famines... Matthew 24:7b KJV

Chapter Six
Understanding Revelation's Mysteries

S E A L 3	see. And I beheld, and lo a black horse; and he that sat on him had a pair of balances in his hand. And I heard a voice in the midst of the four beasts say, A measure of wheat for a penny, and three measures of barley for a penny; and see thou hurt not the oil and the wine. Revelation 6:5-6 KJV	
S E A L 4	And when he had opened the fourth seal, I heard the voice of the fourth beast say, Come and see. And I looked, and behold a pale horse: and his name that sat on him was Death, and Hell followed with him. And power was given unto them over the fourth part of the earth, to kill with sword, and with hunger, and with death, and with the beasts of the earth. Revelation 6:7-8 KJV	...and pestilences, and earthquakes, in divers places. Matthew 24:7 KJV
S E A L 5	And when he had opened the fifth seal, I saw under the altar the souls of them that were slain for the word of God, and for the testimony which they held: Revelation 6:9 KJV	Then shall they deliver you up to be afflicted, and shall kill you: and ye shall be hated of all nations for my name's sake. Matthew 24:9 KJV

The Three Woes
A Guide To Understanding Revelation and End Time Prophecies

Now that we have established the correlation between the warnings from Jesus and the seals, we can now discover the correlation between the seals and recent history. During the late 1800s a number of things occurred that really got the era of great deception off the ground. One was Charles Darwin and his theory of evolution. Since its introduction, this theory has become the cornerstone of what many people believe. The other thing that took place was the establishment of several Christian like organizations that didn't adhere to the true teachings of the Bible. They were the Mormon Church, the Jehovah's Witnesses and the Christian Scientists.

The next event after deception that Jesus warned us to watch for was wars and rumors of wars. So what took place not too long following the turn of the century? That's right, World War 1 and then it was followed not too many years later by World War 2. So, these two events look like a pretty good match for the opening of the second seal and the appearance of the red horse. The event following deception and war is famines that arrived with the rider of the black horse. It is estimated that more than seventy million people died of famine during the twentieth century. That is more deaths by famine than in any other century in history. Pestilences are the events that correspond with the fourth seal and the rider of the pale horse. The twentieth century saw several hundred million deaths due to smallpox. It also saw a pandemic of aids and HIV infections. Another thing that we must be aware of is that the opening of the seals is cumulative. When the second seal was opened, the deception that was released with opening of the first seal didn't cease. In fact, the deception, the wars, the famines and the pestilences are all still ongoing, even though we are in the midst of the work of the fifth seal.

We only briefly covered the first four seals here and their relationship to Jesus' Olivet discourse. To thoroughly prove the

Chapter Six
Understanding Revelation's Mysteries

correlation would require a book unto itself. In fact, there is a book that does an excellent job of dealing with this very relationship as well as proving that most of the seals are now history. The book is "*The Seven Seals in Prophecy and in History*" by Randy Wills. It provides an excellent in depth look at all seven seals.

The Fifth Seal - Persecution

And when he had opened the fifth seal, I saw under the altar the souls of them that were slain for the word of God, and for the testimony which they held: 10 And they cried with a loud voice, saying, How long, O Lord, holy and true, dost thou not judge and avenge our blood on them that dwell on the earth? 11 And white robes were given unto every one of them; and it was said unto them, that they should rest yet for a little season, until their fellowservants also and their brethren, that should be killed as they were, should be fulfilled.
Revelation 6:9-11 KJV

Many in our American society are completely unaware that there is any ongoing persecution of the Christian church in the world today. But as we compare that concept of a world without Christian persecution with the facts from sources that track the actual numbers, a different truth emerges.

According to Pope Benedict XVI, Christians are the most persecuted group in the contemporary world. The Vatican has reported that over 100,000 Christians are violently killed each year because of their faith. According to the World Evangelical Alliance, over 200 million Christians are denied fundamental human rights solely because of their faith. [1]

The Three Woes
A Guide To Understanding Revelation and End Time Prophecies

It is estimated that 100–200 million Christians are alleged to be under assault due to their faith and the majority of these are being persecuted in Muslim dominated nations. Paul Vallely has said that Christians suffer numerically more than any other group in the world today. Of the world's three largest religions, Christians are allegedly the most persecuted with 80% of all acts of religious discrimination being directed at Christians who make up only 33% of the world's population. [1]

A recent 2020 report by Open Doors USA estimates that persecution is now affecting 260 million Christians around the world. In the year 2019, according to Open Doors USA, 9,488 Christian churches or church buildings were attacked, 2,983 Christians were killed for faith related reasons and 3,711 Christians were detained without trial, arrested, sentenced and imprisoned.

A report commissioned by the British foreign secretary Jeremy Hunt and published in May 2019 stated that the level and nature of persecution of Christians in the Middle East "is arguably coming close to meeting the international definition of genocide, according to that adopted by the UN." [1] According to the BBC News Online, Christian persecution is "at near genocide levels." Many Christians are being systematically exterminated and Christian churches burned in predominantly Muslim countries. Although all deaths are not by beheading, many are. We are obviously not through the fifth seal and on to the sixth seal yet, but the facts certainly allow for the contention that we are currently in the midst of the fifth seal.

[1] Ref. Christian Persecution - https://en.wikipedia.org/wiki/Persecution_of_Christians

Chapter Six
Understanding Revelation's Mysteries

The Sixth Seal

And I beheld when he had opened the sixth seal, and, lo, there was a great earthquake; and the sun became black as sackcloth of hair, and the moon became as blood; 13 And the stars of heaven fell unto the earth, even as a fig tree casteth her untimely figs, when she is shaken of a mighty wind. 14 And the heaven departed as a scroll when it is rolled together; and every mountain and island were moved out of their places. 15 And the kings of the earth, and the great men, and the rich men, and the chief captains, and the mighty men, and every bondman, and every free man, hid themselves in the dens and in the rocks of the mountains; 16 And said to the mountains and rocks, Fall on us, and hide us from the face of him that sitteth on the throne, and from the wrath of the Lamb: 17 For the great day of his wrath is come; and who shall be able to stand?

Revelation 6:12-17 KJV

The sixth seal sees a great many things taking place, but before we delve into any of these, there is another issue to cover first. Many readers are probably asking the following question, "How do we know that this is the rapture of the church at Jesus' first coming and not His return to earth at the Battle of Armageddon?" That is a great and very important question. After all, things on the earth are looking pretty bad in Verses 12 through 17 of Revelation Chapter 6. So how do we answer this? Let's look at the following verses from the Book of Revelation.

And I saw three unclean spirits like frogs come out of the mouth of the dragon, and out of the mouth of the beast, and out of the mouth of the false prophet. 14 For they are the spirits of devils, working miracles, which go forth unto

The Three Woes
A Guide To Understanding Revelation and End Time Prophecies

> *the kings of the earth and of the whole world, to gather them to the battle of that great day of God Almighty. 15 Behold, I come as a thief. Blessed is he that watcheth, and keepeth his garments, lest he walk naked, and they see his shame. 16 And he gathered them together into a place called in the Hebrew tongue Armageddon.*
> **Revelation 16:13-16 KJV**

As we look at these versus, the first thing we must remember is that back in chapter two of this book, we established that the Book of Revelation is a sequential and contiguous account of what John saw. These verse place us ten chapters beyond Chapter 6 and much has happened during the intervening chapters. What we first see in the verses above are three unclean spirits emerging from the mouth of the dragon, the mouth of the beast and from the mouth of the false prophet. The dragon is Satan, the beast is the antichrist and the false prophet is the worlds' religious leader.

> *And the great dragon was cast out, that old serpent, called the Devil, and Satan, which deceiveth the whole world: he was cast out into the earth, and his angels were cast out with him.*
> **Revelation 12:9 KJV**

Continuing our look at these verses, the next thing we see is that these leaders are influencing the leaders of the whole world to gather for a battle against God Almighty. Notice that the day of the battle is called the "great day of God Almighty," we are going to deal with this a little later. In Verse 15 we find the words of Jesus Himself, where He says He is coming as a thief and then in Verse 16 we are told that the battle will take place at a location called Armageddon. This is overwhelmingly substantial evidence that these verses in Chapter 16 of Revelation are the Battle of

Chapter Six
Understanding Revelation's Mysteries

Armageddon and that the sixth seal of Chapter 6 in Revelation is the rapture of the church.

Now that we have clarified that the sixth seal is not the Battle of Armageddon, let's move on with our examination of the sixth seal and see what we can learn. The first item we are presented with is a great earthquake. This ought to be of major interest to us. We live in a time where the intensity and frequency of earthquakes are definitely on the rise. Jesus prophesied and warned us that this would be the case just before the end of the church age, but this earthquake seems to have special significance. The scriptures seem to imply that this earthquake is so extreme that it is the cause of the sun being darkened and the moon looking like blood.

The next thing we see is the stars of heaven falling to earth. It is extremely doubtful that these stars that are being referenced are the heavenly bodies that we and other stargazers enjoy viewing at night. Check out the verse from Isaiah below where Isaiah said the constellations would not give their light. They are much more likely to be manmade stars, but more about that a little later. When these three events, the sun darkening, the moon turning to blood and the stars falling are found together in the scriptures, they are commonly referred to as the Cosmic Signs.

> *For the stars of heaven and the constellations thereof shall not give their light: the sun shall be darkened in his going forth, and the moon shall not cause her light to shine.*
> **Isaiah 13:10 KJV**

They provide us with a powerful Biblical study tool, in that we can now tie many scriptures together that are all talking about and describing the rapture of the church. One of those verses is found in Joel.

> *And I will shew wonders in the heavens and in the earth, blood, and fire, and pillars of smoke. 31 The sun shall be turned into darkness, and the moon into blood, before the great and the terrible day of the Lord come.*
> **Joel 2:30-31 KJV**

In this verse, we see the sun and the moon mentioned, but the stars are implied with the reference to the blood, and fire, and pillars of smoke. Before the dawn of the nuclear age, pillars of smoke would have been a foreign term to us, but now, we all recognize pillars of smoke as the resultant mushroom cloud from a nuclear explosion. The other phrase that is of interest to us here is "terrible day of the Lord." Remember back in Revelation 16:14 where the Battle of Armageddon was called the "great day of God Almighty?" Joel is telling us that the rapture will occur before that day.

So, you might be thinking that it is a big leap to think of these stars that are falling to earth as Intercontinental Ballistic Missiles, ICBMs. Check out what Zechariah had to say about it in the verses below. Zechariah describes seeing a roll or scroll flying through the air. He even gives us the dimensions which match many of the ICBMs currently in the world today. And what do scrolls and ICBMs' have in common with each other? Writing! Writing is the common feature that probably caused Zechariah to describe what he saw as a flying roll or scroll.

> *Then I turned, and lifted up mine eyes, and looked, and behold a flying roll. 2 And he said unto me, What seest thou? And I answered, I see a flying roll; the length thereof is twenty cubits, and the breadth thereof ten cubits.*
> **Zechariah 5:1-2 KJV**

Chapter Six
Understanding Revelation's Mysteries

So with the falling stars of heaven being pretty clearly identified as ICBMs, let's continue on with our analysis of the opening of the sixth seal. What we see next is the departing of the heavens, and every mountain and island being removed out of their places. Really, just more evidence of a massive nuclear war. Verse 15 tells us that all mankind is trying to hide themselves in dens and rocks of mountains to hide themselves from the face and wrath of the Lamb.

> *For as the lightning cometh out of the east, and shineth even unto the west; so shall also the coming of the Son of man be. 28 For wheresoever the carcase is, there will the eagles be gathered together. 29 Immediately after the tribulation of those days shall the sun be darkened, and the moon shall not give her light, and the stars shall fall from heaven, and the powers of the heavens shall be shaken: 30 And then shall appear the sign of the Son of man in heaven: and then shall all the tribes of the earth mourn, and they shall see the Son of man coming in the clouds of heaven with power and great glory. 31 And he shall send his angels with a great sound of a trumpet, and they shall gather together his elect from the four winds, from one end of heaven to the other.*
> **Matthew 24:27-31 KJV**

These verses from Matthew are from Jesus' own words in the Olivet discourse where He is describing His return to rapture His church. Here as in Revelation, we see the Cosmic Signs. The great news for all true born again believers in Christ is the description of Jesus coming as the lightning from the east to the west just before the events that cause the Cosmic Signs. Jesus says, immediately after the tribulation of those days, the Cosmic Signs will appear. What we can learn from this is that we as Christians should not expect to escape all tribulation. What we will escape is the great tribulation and the wrath of God.

Another fact to notice here is where Jesus says that all the tribes of the earth shall see the Son of man coming in the clouds of heaven. There are those who believe that when the rapture occurs, no one will realize it. They believe the rapture event will be masked as a mass suicide or it will be explained as a mass abduction by aliens or cloaked in some other explainable occurrence, anything that would adequately hide the rapture occurrence. But that is not what Jesus says in His Olivet discourse, where He said all the tribes of the earth shall see the Son of man coming in the clouds. The sixth seal also implies that all mankind is trying to hide from the Lamb.

Before we conclude with the sixth seal, let's take a look at some other scriptures that we can tie to the rapture because of the Cosmic Signs.

> *Multitudes, multitudes in the valley of decision: for the day of the Lord is near in the valley of decision. 15 The sun and the moon shall be darkened, and the stars shall withdraw their shining.*
> **Joel 3:14-15 KJV**

> *Behold, the day of the Lord cometh, cruel both with wrath and fierce anger, to lay the land desolate: and he shall destroy the sinners thereof out of it. 10 For the stars of heaven and the constellations thereof shall not give their light: the sun shall be darkened in his going forth, and the moon shall not cause her light to shine. 11 And I will punish the world for their evil, and the wicked for their iniquity; and I will cause the arrogancy of the proud to cease, and will lay low the haughtiness of the terrible.*

Chapter Six
Understanding Revelation's Mysteries

Isaiah 13:9-11 KJV

Therefore I will shake the heavens, and the earth shall remove out of her place, in the wrath of the Lord of hosts, and in the day of his fierce anger.
Isaiah 13:13 KJV

The earth is utterly broken down, the earth is clean dissolved, the earth is moved exceedingly. 20 The earth shall reel to and fro like a drunkard, and shall be removed like a cottage; and the transgression thereof shall be heavy upon it; and it shall fall, and not rise again.
Isaiah 24:19-20 KJV

As we read these scriptures, a very disturbing picture arises, a picture of a terrible and awesome God who is fiercely angry and ready to pronounce judgment upon an evil and wicked world. The world today can't comprehend a God such as this. As we have said earlier, they have fashioned God into a being of their own perception, one who is only love and peace and pleasantness, one who places no demands upon anyone. This is not who God is. God is good, holy, righteous, faithful and just. He has given us His Word. He has given us His commandments. He is true and faithful to His Word. He can not lie and He demands justice.

Follow peace with all men, and holiness, without which no man shall see the Lord:
Hebrews 12:14 KJV

Now the works of the flesh are manifest, which are these; Adultery, fornication, uncleanness, lasciviousness, 20 Idolatry, witchcraft, hatred, variance, emulations, wrath, strife, seditions, heresies, 21 Envyings, murders, drunkenness, revellings, and such like: of the which I tell

> *you before, as I have also told you in time past, that they which do such things shall not inherit the kingdom of God.*

Galatians 5:19-21 KJV

God gave us His laws and commandments; Jesus died on the cross and shed His blood for the forgiveness of sins for all those who would accept His forgiveness. At the end of the opening of the sixth seal, we see God preparing to pour out His wrath and demand justice from all who rejected His Son's sin offering.

The 144,000 of the Children of Israel

There is very little that we know about the 144,000. There are 12,000 from each of the twelve tribes of Israel who receive the seal of God in their foreheads. This seal appears to provide a protection to all those who were sealed. After they have received their seals at the beginning of Revelation Chapter 7, there isn't any account of the 144,000 until we see them with the Lamb in Revelation 14:1. Since all 144,000 are with the Lamb, it is probably safe to assume that neither the antichrist that kills the two witnesses nor anyone else was able to kill or harm any of these Children of Israel. We can also assume that the saints that the antichrist made war against in Revelation 13:7 were probably converts out of the House of Israel that came from the ministry of these Children of Israel and from the two witnesses.

> *And I saw another angel ascending from the east, having the seal of the living God: and he cried with a loud voice to the four angels, to whom it was given to hurt the earth and the sea, 3 Saying, Hurt not the earth, neither the sea, nor the trees, till we have sealed the servants of our God in their foreheads. 4 And I heard the number of them which*

Chapter Six
Understanding Revelation's Mysteries

> *were sealed: and there were sealed an hundred and forty and four thousand of all the tribes of the children of Israel.*
> **Revelation 7:2-4 KJV**

> *And I looked, and, lo, a Lamb stood on the mount Sion, and with him an hundred forty and four thousand, having his Father's name written in their foreheads.*
> **Revelation 14:1 KJV**

The First Woe - The Locusts with a Scorpion Sting

The first woe begins at Revelation 9:1 where the apostle John sees a star fall from heaven. We are told that this star is an angel and he has the keys to the bottomless pit. As this pit is opened, a smoke arises that darkens the sun and the air, and out of the smoke comes locusts that are given power to sting mankind like a scorpion would sting.

> *And the fifth angel sounded, and I saw a star fall from heaven unto the earth: and to him was given the key of the bottomless pit. 2 And he opened the bottomless pit; and there arose a smoke out of the pit, as the smoke of a great furnace; and the sun and the air were darkened by reason of the smoke of the pit.*
> **Revelation 9:1-2 KJV**

The locusts are commanded not to hurt the earth nor any green thing, but they are commanded to hurt mankind for five months. The pain from these *scorpion* locust stings will be so great that men will desire to die, but we are told that death will escape them.

The Three Woes
A Guide To Understanding Revelation and End Time Prophecies

> *And to them it was given that they should not kill them, but that they should be tormented five months: and their torment was as the torment of a scorpion, when he striketh a man.*
> **Revelation 9:5 KJV**

For the next several verses, Revelation 9:7-11, we are given a very detailed description of what these locusts look like. As we read John's detailed description of these locusts, the most striking and obvious thing that jumps out at us, is the fact that John's description doesn't look anything like a locust. Actually, the only similarity the description has to a locus is that both can fly.

The shapes of the locusts remind John of horses, and on their heads were crowns like gold and the faces were like men. These locusts had breastplates of iron and their wings sounded like chariots running to battle. John tells us that their tails had stingers in them. Looking at this description from our modern day perspective, the description sounds a lot more like an apache helicopter with stinger missiles being piloted by a man wearing a gold helmet than it does a locust.

> *And the shapes of the locusts were like unto horses prepared unto battle; and on their heads were as it were crowns like gold, and their faces were as the faces of men. 8 And they had hair as the hair of women, and their teeth were as the teeth of lions. 9 And they had breastplates, as it were breastplates of iron; and the sound of their wings was as the sound of chariots of many horses running to battle. 10 And they had tails like unto scorpions, and there were stings in their tails: and their power was to hurt men five months.*
> **Revelation 9:7-10 KJV**

Chapter Six
Understanding Revelation's Mysteries

While we don't know for sure what it is that John is seeing, what we do know is that these *scorpion* locusts have the power to torment men for five months. They were released when the fifth trumpet angel sounded proclaiming the first woe in Revelation 9:1. The first woe ends at Revelation 9:12 with the statement "One woe is past." Our big take away here is knowing that each of the next two woes will each cover a time span of three and one half years, for a total of seven years. So John is clearly showing us that this woe must begin five months prior to the beginning of the seven years of tribulation known as Daniel's Seventh Week or the Time of Jacob's Trouble.

> *One woe is past; and, behold, there come two woes more hereafter.*
> **Revelation 9:12 KJV**

The Second Woe - The Two Witnesses

The two witnesses appear at the sounding of the sixth trumpet angel which is the second woe. The second woe begins at Revelation 9:13 with the sounding of the sixth trumpet angel, immediately following the end of the first woe. Even though the apostle John doesn't tell us about the two witnesses until Revelation 11:3, the work and ministry of the two witnesses spans the entire forty two month time frame of the second woe. These forty two months coincide with the first one half of the seven year tribulation period.

We are not told who these two witnesses are. Over the years there has been speculation that they are possibly Elijah and Enoch, or James and John, or Peter and Paul. Another individual that has been mentioned as being one of the two witnesses is Moses. Elijah and Enoch are frequently mentioned as candidates because they were taken up to God and never died. Elijah and

The Three Woes
A Guide To Understanding Revelation and End Time Prophecies

Chart 4

Rev. 8:13 Woe, woe, woe to the inhabiters of the earth because of the three angels yet to sound.

	Angelic Proclamation	Resulting Punishment	
Fifth Angel / 1st Woe	Rev. 9:1 And the fifth angel sounded Rev. 9:2-5 Locusts torment men five months Rev. 9:12 One woe is past.	Rev. 9:2-5 Locusts from the bottomless pit have power to torment men 5 months	Five Months
Sixth Angel / 2nd Woe	Rev. 9:13 And the sixth angel sounded Rev. 9:14-15 Angels kill mankind Rev. 11:2-3 Holy City taken Rev. 11:3-12 Two witnesses Rev. 11:14 The second woe is past	Rev. 9:14-15 Four angels from Euphrates river to slay a third of men for an hour, and a day, and a month and a year Rev. 11:2-3 The holy city shall be tread under foot by the gentiles for forty two months Rev. 11:3-12 My two witnesses shall prophecy a thousand two hundred and three score days	3.5 years
Seventh Angel / 3rd Woe	Rev. 11:15 The seventh angel sounded Rev. 12:6 Woman flees to wilderness Rev. 12:13-14 Serpent persecutes woman Rev. 13:1-7 The beast makes war with the saints Rev. 16:17 It is done. (3rd Woe past)	Rev. 12:6 The woman flees to the wilderness for a thousand two hundred and three score days. Rev. 12:13-14 The serpent (dragon) persecutes the woman for a time, and times and half a time Rev. 13:1-7 The beast makes war with the saints for forty two months and over comes them	3.5 years

The Seven Years of Jacob's Trouble

Moses are often mentioned because, when they were on the earth, they performed similar miracles as the two witnesses will

Chapter Six
Understanding Revelation's Mysteries

perform. Elijah and the apostle John seem like they could be potential candidates because of two scripture verses, one about Elijah in Malachi and the other about the apostle John in Revelation.

> *Behold, I will send you Elijah the prophet before the coming of the great and dreadful day of the Lord:*
> **Malachi 4:5**

> *And I took the little book out of the angel's hand, and ate it up; and it was in my mouth sweet as honey: and as soon as I had eaten it, my belly was bitter. 11 And he said unto me, Thou must prophesy again before many peoples, and nations, and tongues, and kings.*
> **Revelation 10:10-11 KJV**

Based on these two scriptures, Elijah and the apostle John seem to be the most scripturally logical candidates, but who the individuals turn out to be really doesn't matter. What does matter is that the world is in a terrible mess at this point in time. The church has been removed from the earth in the rapture and the people who remain upon the earth have just gone through being tormented five months by the sting of the scorpion locusts. Now, the people of earth are facing what appears to be some type of war or battle that will take place during the forty two month time frame of this second woe where four angels are loosed to kill a third of mankind. Based on today's world population, that would mean more than two billion deaths.

> *And the four angels were loosed, which were prepared for an hour, and a day, and a month, and a year, for to slay the third part of men.*
> **Revelation 9:15 KJV**

The Three Woes
A Guide To Understanding Revelation and End Time Prophecies

The length of this war that is described in Revelation 9:15 is not thirteen months and one day. The scripture says it was prepared for this specific day. It most likely lasts for the entire forty two months of this trumpet angel's woe. As this forty two month battle is taking place, the two witnesses are prophesying and working miracles on the earth trying to turn mans' attention toward God. There will be men that will try to take the life of these two witnesses, but they will fail. The scripture tells us that fire will proceed out of the mouth of the two witnesses and will devour any enemies that try to kill them. Finally, at the end of the forty two months, the beast from the bottomless pit will make war with the two witnesses and will kill them. There are several beasts mentioned in the Book of Revelation, but the scripture doesn't clearly tell us which beast this is. It is probably safe to assume that this beast is the antichrist. We know from other scripture that the antichrist will be on the scene at the beginning of this forty two month time frame because of his involvement with the Israeli peace agreement that marks the beginning of the seven years of tribulation. We also see that the antichrist doesn't seem to display all of his true demonic nature until the middle of the seven years. The killing of these two witnesses and the desecration of the third Jewish temple seem to culminate in his complete submission to total demonic possession and control.

> *And if any man will hurt them, fire proceedeth out of their mouth, and devoureth their enemies: and if any man will hurt them, he must in this manner be killed.*
> **Revelation 11:5 KJV**

> *And when they shall have finished their testimony, the beast that ascendeth out of the bottomless pit shall make war against them, and shall overcome them, and kill them.*
> **Revelation 11:7 KJV**

Chapter Six
Understanding Revelation's Mysteries

Following the deaths of these two witnesses, their bodies will lie in the street for three and one half days. During this time, the people of the earth will rejoice and will send gifts to one another in celebration of their deaths. This sounds a lot like Christmas. Whether this event might occur during the Christmas season or at another time is unknown. What we do know is at the end of the three and one half days, the Spirit of life from God enters into the two witnesses and a voice from heaven tells them to "come up hither." At Revelation 11:14, we are told the "second woe is past." This marks the half way point of the seven years of tribulation.

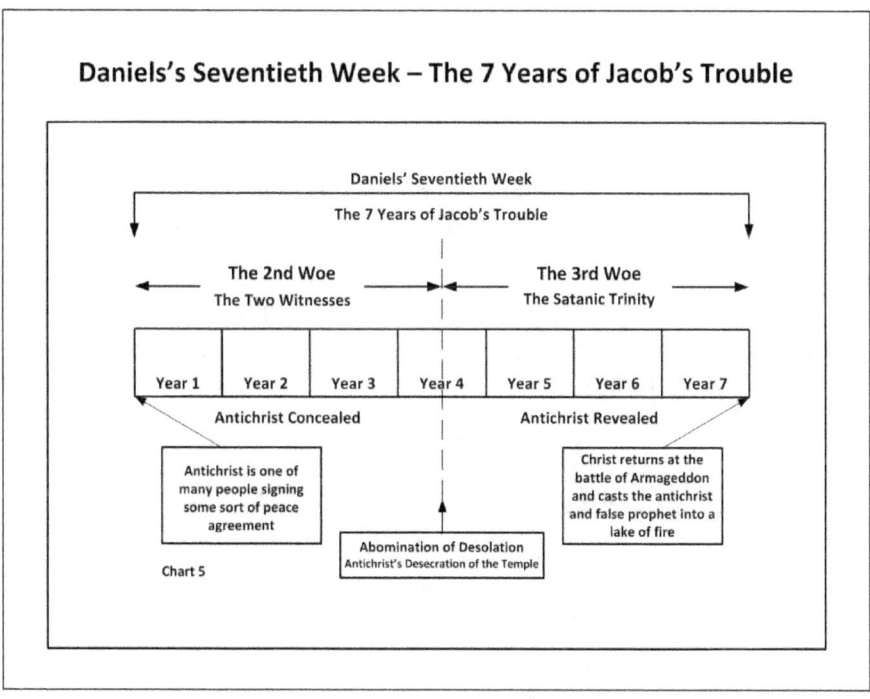

And they of the people and kindreds and tongues and nations shall see their dead bodies three days and an half, and shall not suffer their dead bodies to be put in graves. 10 And they that dwell upon the earth shall rejoice over them, and make merry, and shall send gifts one to another;

> *because these two prophets tormented them that dwelt on the earth. 11 And after three days and an half the Spirit of life from God entered into them, and they stood upon their feet; and great fear fell upon them which saw them. 12 And they heard a great voice from heaven saying unto them, Come up hither. And they ascended up to heaven in a cloud; and their enemies beheld them.*
> **Revelation 11:9-12 KJV**

The Third Woe - The Satanic Trinity

The Satanic Trinity as we will call it is an example of where Satan is trying to imitate God. The third woe begins at Revelation 11:15, with the sounding of the seventh trumpet angel. Here, we find Satan preparing to ready his forces and his chosen leaders to do battle against God and His saints. There are three main characters described here with this third woe, they are: (1) the dragon, who is Satan, (2) the first beast, who is the antichrist, and (3) a second beast, who is the false prophet. We know that the dragon is Satan by reading Revelation 20:2.

> **NOTE:** The person of the antichrist is an individual who will oppose Christ and substitute himself in Christ's place before Christ's Second Coming. The word "antichrist" is not used in the Book of Revelation. In fact it is only found four times in the Bible: in 1 John 2:18, 1 John 2:22, 1 John 4:3 and 2 John 1:7. In each of these occurrences, it seems to refer more to a spirit than to a specific individual. The concept of the antichrist as a specific individual finds its origin in the Book of Daniel Chapter 7.
>
> *And the ten horns out of this kingdom are ten kings that shall arise: and another shall rise after them; and he shall*

Chapter Six
Understanding Revelation's Mysteries

be diverse from the first, and he shall subdue three kings. And he shall speak great words against the most High, and shall wear out the saints of the most High, and think to change times and laws: and they shall be given into his hand until a time and times and the dividing of time.
Daniel 7:24-25 KJV

And he laid hold on the dragon, that old serpent, which is the Devil, and Satan, and bound him a thousand years,
Revelation 20:2 KJV

The term beast is used 44 times in the King James Version of the Book of Revelation. During the course of the Book of Revelation, the term beast is often describing different individuals or in some cases, different things. Until one begins to really study the book, the use of this one term can be quite confusing. For the current part of our study, we are going to limit our discussion to those beasts described in the third woe.

In Revelation 13:1-8, we see a beast being described. As this beast is initially being described, it appears to be an alliance or block of nations. We are told that this beast has seven heads and ten horns. There is much speculation on the meaning of these heads and horns.

Are they seven kings ruling together over ten kingdoms? That is what it seems, but we don't know for certain. What we do know is this beast will gain great power over the world and that power is derived from the dragon or Satan. We also see that one of the heads of this beast is wounded to the point that it should die, but it appears to be miraculously healed. This is another attempt by Satan to imitate God, where Jesus died and rose again. Don't be confused, the scriptures don't tell us that the wound was a head wound, but that one of the seven heads was wounded.

> *And the beast which I saw was like unto a leopard, and his feet were as the feet of a bear, and his mouth as the mouth of a lion: and the dragon gave him his power, and his seat, and great authority. 3 And I saw one of his heads as it were wounded to death; and his deadly wound was healed: and all the world wondered after the beast.*
> **Revelation 13:2-3 KJV**

At this point the description of the beast seems to change such that we no longer see the beast as a seven nation alliance. The head that was miraculously healed appears to become the leader of this block of nations. The biblical scriptures call this individual the antichrist. Instead of seeing seven heads, we now see one head of this beast become the leader of the seven nation alliance that has been consolidated and united into a powerful force led by this individual we call the antichrist. His power will be given to him for forty two months; this is the second half of the seven year tribulation period. During his time in power, he will make war against the saints of God, those converts from the ministry of the 144,000.

> *And there was given unto him a mouth speaking great things and blasphemies; and power was given unto him to continue forty and two months.*
> **Revelation 13:5 KJV**

> *And it was given unto him to make war with the saints, and to overcome them: and power was given him over all kindreds, and tongues, and nations.*
> **Revelation 13:7 KJV**

As we move on to Revelation 13:11, we find the second beast, the false prophet. We are told that this second beast has power like the first beast and that his power is also derived from the dragon,

Chapter Six
Understanding Revelation's Mysteries

the devil. One of the chief characteristics of the false prophet is that he has the power to deceive them that dwell on the earth. We are told that he has the power and influence to cause men to worship the first beast, the antichrist. The first beast, the antichrist, receives a wound by a sword so severe that it either causes death or it should have caused death. We don't know for sure which it is, but most likely, the wound causes the death of the antichrist. We are told that the antichrist is healed, but we are not told how he is healed or by whom he is healed. However, since we are dealing with demonic spirits here, it would probably be a fairly safe assumption that the false prophet will be the one who will heal the antichrist by demonic means.

> *And I beheld another beast coming up out of the earth; and he had two horns like a lamb, and he spake as a dragon. 12 And he exerciseth all the power of the first beast before him, and causeth the earth and them which dwell therein to worship the first beast, whose deadly wound was healed. 13 And he doeth great wonders, so that he maketh fire come down from heaven on the earth in the sight of men, 14 And deceiveth them that dwell on the earth by the means of those miracles which he had power to do in the sight of the beast; saying to them that dwell on the earth, that they should make an image to the beast, which had the wound by a sword, and did live.*
> **Revelation 13:11-14 KJV**

Soon after the antichrist is healed, the false prophet quickly decides to have an image made of the antichrist that was healed. The false prophet has the power to give life to that image and to cause that image to speak. Animatronics and artificial intelligence may be at work here. The false prophet then commands that all who refuse to worship the image of the antichrist, to be killed. The false prophet next causes all the people of the earth to receive a mark in their right hand or their forehead. He further decrees that no one can buy or sell without the mark of the beast. The "mark of the beast" is a term frequently used in some churches and various Christian circles, but we are actually told that all who worship the beast will receive one of three symbols to indicate that they had bowed to the image of the beast and pledged their worship of the beast. We are told that the individual who is willing to worship the beast to escape a sentence of death will either receive the mark of the beast, the name of the beast or the number of the name of the beast in either their right hand or forehead.

> *And he had power to give life unto the image of the beast, that the image of the beast should both speak, and cause that as many as would not worship the image of the beast should be killed. 16 And he causeth all, both small and great, rich and poor, free and bond, to receive a mark in their right hand, or in their foreheads: 17 And that no man might buy or sell, save he that had the mark, or the name of the beast, or the number of his name.*
> **Revelation 13:15-17 KJV**

Upon first hearing of this decree, one might think so what, I'll be killed if I don't bow and worship the beast and his image, so I'll just bow and do it. I can't exist without being able to buy and sell anyway, so I'll just bow and take the mark and go on my merry way. We live in a world where we have grown accustom to people not keeping their word or keeping their promises. We see it all the time in political battles. A campaigner will make a promise to get elected and it seems the promise is long forgotten before the election results are even counted. The trouble is, this is an all or nothing situation. If you don't bow to worship the beast and take the mark of the beast, then the satanic trinity is going to take your life. If you do bow to worship and take the mark of the beast, then

Chapter Six
Understanding Revelation's Mysteries

Almighty God is going to make note and remember. Once the satanic trio's forty two months of power has come to an end, the dragon will be cast into the bottomless pit and the antichrist and false prophet will be cast into the lake of fire. All who bowed to worship the beast and took the mark of the beast are doomed to eternal punishment by God and banishment from God.

> *And the third angel followed them, saying with a loud voice, If any man worship the beast and his image, and receive his mark in his forehead, or in his hand, 10 The same shall drink of the wine of the wrath of God, which is poured out without mixture into the cup of his indignation; and he shall be tormented with fire and brimstone in the presence of the holy angels, and in the presence of the Lamb: 11 And the smoke of their torment ascendeth up for ever and ever: and they have no rest day nor night, who worship the beast and his image, and whosoever receiveth the mark of his name.*
> **Revelation 14:9-11 KJV**

So now that we have determined that it is eternally important that the mark not be taken, how do we recognize that mark? First and foremost, one should make sure that they have repented of their sins and are living for Christ, for all who are born again will not face this dilemma. They will be removed from the earth when Christ returns for His church several years prior to this time. For those who remain on earth, the first indication that the mark of the beast is involved is the requirement to worship the beast and his image. As we read the scripture, it indicates that the real requirement is to worship the beast and the receiving of the mark of the beast is only the indication that someone has complied. So based on this understanding, the mark of the beast probably won't be implemented until the antichrist is revealed and the image of the beast has been created.

The Three Woes
A Guide To Understanding Revelation and End Time Prophecies

Here is wisdom. Let him that hath understanding count the number of the beast: for it is the number of a man; and his number is Six hundred threescore and six.
Revelation 13:18 KJV

Once the image of the beast is available, the mark of the beast will be revealed. Through the years, people have looked at numerous numbering systems and wondered if they were the system that is spoken of in Revelation. In the past, most systems wouldn't meet the numerical requirement of being able to count the seven plus billion people on earth. The United States social security system is only capable of numbering to one billion with its nine digits. Some other systems have comparable limitations while others like India could number up to a trillion people with their twelve digit numbering system.

Many have speculated over the years about this number, but we have few clues as to what it will be. We can safely assume that the numbering system must be capable of numbering everyone in the world, so that probably means a system that can handle numbers larger than ten billion. We are told that it will be the number of the beast, whose number is 666 which is also the number of a man. So we might ask what number is associated with a man. A potential future world ID number, a telephone number or the number contained within ones residential address where the street, city and state make it unique are potential candidates.

Currently, we simply don't know for sure what the numbering system will be. One new technology that has arrived on the scene a few decades ago looks like it could be a key player in the "mark of the beast" system. That system is called RFID, or Radio Frequency Identification. The concept for this technology was introduced in the 1940s and it has been in commercial development since the mid 1980s. Its use as a commercially viable product has pushed the RFID technology market to over twenty billion dollars in 2020.

RFID tags can be attached to cash, clothing, and possessions, or implanted in animals and people. In major industrialized societies around the world, RFID is being used to track products, pharmaceuticals, livestock, pets and even humans. To do this, the RFID device contains a tiny radio transponder, which is a radio receiver and transmitter. To do all of this, you might think the RFID device would be somewhat large, and for some implementations this would be true. But in other implementations the product has been miniaturized to the size of a grain of rice. Many of us already have RFID technology in products we use and may not even know it. Some credit cards today don't need to be inserted into a reader, but can simply be swiped near the reader and the reader grabs the info wirelessly. All United States passports issued since 2007 have RFID chips embedded in the front cover.

When the RFID has been miniaturized to the size of a grain of rice and inserted into an animal or a human, it is generally called a microchip implant. These implants can be used to assign a unique number or identifier to an individual; to replace house, work and car keys or car key FOBs; to provide security access to restricted areas; to record and track important medical information; and to buy and sell products with automatic bank account debiting and crediting capability. A GPS-enabled chip could one day make it possible for individuals to be physically located by latitude, longitude, altitude, and velocity. A true 1984 24/7 big brother tracking device.

Another technology that burst upon the scene shortly after the start of the 21st century is digital currencies. Bitcoin is a decentralized cryptocurrency, or digital currency, without a central bank or a single administrator that was created by a private individual or group of individuals. Since Bitcoin was created, there have been a number of other private, meaning non-government backed, digital currencies that have emerged. Currently many countries are looking at digital currencies as a replacement for paper money but only twenty some are experimenting with them.

Another piece of the puzzle that is just now exploding onto the scene is ID2020 and its connection to a vaccine for the COVID virus. Microsoft Technology Licensing, LLC (*Bill Gates, founder of Microsoft*) has applied for a patent called "Cryptocurrency System Using Body Activity Data." It is described in Publication Number WO/2020/060606 and may be viewed at the WEB address listed below. It uses quantum dot technology to create a tattoo on the skin. Bill Gates is advocating that every person in the world **must** be vaccinated against the COVID virus.

https://patentscope.wipo.int/search/en/detail.jsf?docId=WO2020060606

It would seem logical that the "mark of the beast" might involve some type of merged product consisting of an RFID microchip and/or a micro dot vaccine and a digital currency issued by the government of the antichrist.

What we do know is that the power of the satanic trinity is going to cease at the end of their forty two month reign of terror. Christ will return to the earth with His army, the raptured church. Christ and the antichrist will battle in a place called Armageddon. Christ and His army will be victorious and the antichrist and the false prophet will both be cast alive into a lake of fire.

Chapter Six
Understanding Revelation's Mysteries

And he gathered them together into a place called in the Hebrew tongue Armageddon.
Revelation 16:16 KJV

And the beast was taken, and with him the false prophet that wrought miracles before him, with which he deceived them that had received the mark of the beast, and them that worshipped his image. These both were cast alive into a lake of fire burning with brimstone.
Revelation 19:20 KJV

And he laid hold on the dragon, that old serpent, which is the Devil, and Satan, and bound him a thousand years, 3 And cast him into the bottomless pit, and shut him up, and set a seal upon him, that he should deceive the nations no more, till the thousand years should be fulfilled: and after that he must be loosed a little season.
Revelation 20:2-3 KJV

As we said earlier, we are not clearly told when the seventh trumpet angel, the third woe, is finished. That is most likely because of the seven vial or bowl judgment angels, since their ministry begins during the time of the seventh trumpet angel's judgment but continues on after its conclusion. What we are told in Revelation 16:17 is "It is done." The only thing we see following this statement and before the Marriage Supper of the Lamb is the impact of the seventh vial/bowl judgment.

Who Is The Antichrist

In Christian eschatology, antichrist is any person or spirit that opposes Christ, whereas **THE** Antichrist is a principal character in the Bible who becomes the ultimate enemy of Christ and opposition to His followers. To best determine who the antichrist is, or will be, we should probably start by looking at how the Bible describes him. As we have said earlier, the word antichrist is not used in the Book of the Revelation and is only found four times in the Bible. The Bible, however, has a lot to say about a particular individual who fills this roll of being the ultimate enemy of Christ. Most of the foundation describing this person is found in the Old Testament Book of Daniel, while in the Book of Revelation we are provided with a more detailed look at what this dictators brief time in power will look like. So what are the characteristics of this individual that set him apart from any other individual that has an antichrist spirit?

	Characteristics of the Antichrist
1	The antichrist Will Blaspheme God
2	The antichrist Will Display Miraculous Powers
3	The antichrist Will Claim to be God and will be Worshiped
4	The antichrist Comes Back to Life
5	The antichrist Rules in Full Authority
6	The antichrist Will Control the World's Economy
7	The antichrist Desecrates God's Temple
8	The antichrist Will Attempt to Destroy Israel
9	The antichrist Will Cause Earth's Armies to Fight Against Christ
10	The antichrist's Final Destiny is to be cast into the Lake of Fire

Most of these major characteristics won't be obvious until after the antichrist rises to power during the closing three and one half years of the great tribulation. So what are some characteristics that we could expect to see before that time? The individual may or may not be Jewish. There are arguments both ways. It seems initially that the antichrist may claim to be the messiah which would require him to be Jewish, but then he will fight against Israel, showing clearly that he is not the messiah and possibly not Jewish. He is likely to be a very charismatic, attractive and

Chapter Six
Understanding Revelation's Mysteries

probably a widely popular diplomat. He will be an individual who can easily influence the masses and persuade many to follow his leadership.

These are not very individualistic descriptions, but rather broad descriptions that could be applicable to many political leaders around the world. We do know, from the Book of Daniel, that the antichrist will confirm a covenant for one week (*seven years*). This covenant or peace treaty, as it has been called, will be between Israel and her enemies. The signing of this agreement marks the start of the seven years of tribulation and is the only true defining characteristic prior to his rise to power. The following table lists some individuals who the world has seen as potential candidates for the title of antichrist.

> *And he shall confirm the covenant with many for one week: and in the midst of the week he shall cause the sacrifice and the oblation to cease, and for the overspreading of abominations he shall make it desolate, even until the consummation, and that determined shall be poured upon the desolate.*
> **Daniel 9:27 KJV**

Candidate For Antichrist Office/Position	Reasons For	Reasons Against
Nero Caesar Roman Caesar	Head of the old Roman Empire after which the New World Order will be patterned.	Deceased.
Napoleon Bonaparte Emperor of France	As French emperor, held one of the most powerful	Deceased.

The Three Woes
A Guide To Understanding Revelation and End Time Prophecies

	positions in the world.	
Adolf Hitler Chancellor of Germany	A very charismatic Individual. Led the nations of the world into World War Two. Tried to exterminate the Jewish people.	Deceased.
The American President	As a USA president, holds one of the most powerful positions in the world.	Most presidents don't come close to meeting the characteristics and America is not part of a seven nation alliance.
The Catholic Pope	Holds one of the most powerful religious positions in the world.	Most popes don't come close to meeting the characteristics. Due to his religious position he would be a better candidate for False Prophet
Henry Kissinger Statesman and advisor to the USA President	He is Jewish. Assisted with several Israeli and Palestinian peace agreements.	Deceased.
Mikhail Gorbachev President of USSR	As president of the USSR, held one of the most	Deceased.

Chapter Six
Understanding Revelation's Mysteries

	powerful positions in the world.	
Barack Obama President of America	A very charismatic Individual. As a USA president, held one of the most powerful positions in the world.	No longer president of the USA. The USA is not part of a seven nation alliance. Is not currently part of any peace discussions.
George Soros	He is Jewish.	He is 94 years of age.
Recep Erdogan President of Turkey	He claims to be God.	Currently he doesn't seem to have an interest in negotiating a peace agreement between Israel and the Palestinians.
Donald Trump President of America	Holds one of the most powerful positions in the world. Is the one pushing the "Deal of the Century" between Israel and the Palestinians.	USA is not currently a part of a seven nation alliance.
Jared Kushner Investor, Advisor to USA President	Is the lead framer of the current peace agreement	Doesn't currently appear to be on the verge of

	between Israel and the Palestinians, called the 'Deal of the Century'. Owns Kushner Companies whose headquarters and address were at 666 Fifth Ave. NY, NY. He is Jewish.	becoming a leading member of a seven nation alliance.

So, can we say who the antichrist is? No way! What we do see is that people have been guessing for years and the church will most probably be removed from the earth before the true identity of the antichrist is revealed.

Who Is The False Prophet

Often, we tend to think of a false prophet as one who predicts the future inaccurately. A false prophet is really anyone who represents false gods or who claims to speak for God, but instead is spreading false messages and false teachings. Being a false predictor of the future may not even be part of a false prophet's work. Jesus warned us, in His sermon on the mount, that there would be many false prophets. What we see in Revelation Chapter 13 is the ultimate false prophet. He will be the one who will receive super natural power from the devil to augment the antichrist's rise to power. The false prophet in Revelation will be a specific individual who will point the whole world to worship another man, the first beast, the antichrist.

Chapter Six
Understanding Revelation's Mysteries

And many false prophets shall rise, and shall deceive many.
Matthew 24:11 KJV

And I beheld another beast coming up out of the earth; and he had two horns like a lamb, and he spake as a dragon. 12 And he exerciseth all the power of the first beast before him, and causeth the earth and them which dwell therein to worship the first beast, whose deadly wound was healed.
Revelation 13:11-12 KJV

False prophets are becoming more prominent in today's age of tolerance and rebellion against God. Most however, will be leaders of relatively small groups of people usually numbering no more than a few hundred and at the most a few thousand. So how will we recognize **THE** False Prophet? As opposed to the many false prophets that Jesus referred to in Matthew Chapter 24, this false prophet will lead a mass of people that will likely number into the millions or billions. As opposed to the antichrist, there is not a long list of contenders for this title. Through the years there have been a hand full of names that have been mentioned but all quickly fell into obscurity. The one exception is the office of the pope.

What has partially driven this is the prophecy of St. Malachy, who was the archbishop of Armagh, Ireland in the 1100s. While Malachy's prophecy is not scriptural cannon, it has seemed to endure through the years, albeit with significant detractors. St. Malachy claimed to have a vision while visiting Rome. In his vision, he claimed to receive a short description of each pope that would be over the Catholic Church. His vision resulted in a list of 112 popes in succession, with the 112th pope being the final pope. It is claimed that the record of St. Malachy's vision was recorded and

The Three Woes
A Guide To Understanding Revelation and End Time Prophecies

deposited in the Vatican's Secret Archives and forgotten until its rediscovery there in 1590.

St. Malachy's vision seemed to lay dormant until 2005 when someone noticed that Pope John Paul II was the 110th pope since St. Malachy's prophecy. That meant that if the prophecy was true, then Pope Benedict XVI would be the last pope before the final 112th pope. In 2013 Pope Benedict XVI resigned and Pope Francis became the 112th pope. Will Pope Francis turnout to be the false prophet of Revelation Chapter 13? We don't know, but his coziness with the Muslim religion and his desire to be inclusive to all people are causing many to watch closely.

Note: With the death of Pope Francis in April of 2025 and the election of Pope Leo XIV as the 113th pope since St. Malachy's prediction, this prophecy should be considered debunk.

Internet links to some current articles along with the articles headline and the author are provided below for your review. We will leave it to the reader to form their own conclusion.

Internet Link	https://www.nowtheendbegins.com/catholic-muslim-interfaith-council-created-by-pope-francis-announces-new-chrislam-headquarters-in-2022-that-combines-mosque-church/
Headline	The Catholic-Muslim Interfaith Council Created By Pope Francis Announces New Chrislam Headquarters Opening In 2022 That Combines A Mosque And Church According To Signed Covenant
Author/ Date	by Geoffrey Grider / September 22, 2019
Internet	https://www.nowtheendbegins.com/end-times-

Chapter Six
Understanding Revelation's Mysteries

Link	covenant-pope-francis-antichrist-signed-islamic-leader-makes-no-reference-to-jesus-christ/
Headline	IN THE NAME OF ALLAH: The End Times "Universal Peace Document" Pope Francis Signed With Islamic Leader Makes No Reference Of Any Kind To Jesus Christ Or The Bible
Author/Date	by Geoffrey Grider / February 25, 2019
Internet Link	https://www.theaustralian.com.au/nation/world/unholy-row-war-of-words-over-popes-and-grand-imams-declaration-of-fraternity/news-story/2306cf31e6698fe149c83ad9cf607d04
Headline	Unholy row: War of words over Pope's and Grand Imam's declaration of fraternity
Author/Date	By Tess Livingstone / February 13, 2019
Internet Link	https://www.ncronline.org/news/quick-reads/us-catholic-officials-welcome-catholic-muslim-document-signed-pope
Headline	U.S. Catholic officials welcome Catholic-Muslim document signed by pope
Author/Date	by Catholic News Service / Feb 8, 2019
Internet Link	https://www.breakingisraelnews.com/145012/pope-pushes-one-world-religion-on-israels-independence-day/
Headline	Pope Pushes One World Religion on Israel's Independence Day
Author/Date	By Adam Eliyahu Berkowitz February 11, 2020

The Three Woes
A Guide To Understanding Revelation and End Time Prophecies

Internet Link	http://unexplainedmysteriesoftheworld.com/archives/the-vatican-has-just-released-a-new-chrislam-logo-for-the-popes-upcoming-interfaith-visit-to-morocco
Headline	The Vatican Has Just Released A New "Chrislam Logo" For The Pope's Upcoming Interfaith Visit To Morocco
Author/ Date	By Michael Snyder / Unexplained Mysteries Of The World 2020
Internet Link	https://cnsnews.com/blog/michael-w-chapman/archbishop-jan-lenga-pope-francis-usurper-and-heretic-leading-world-astray
Headline	Archbishop Jan Lenga: Pope Francis is "Usurper and Heretic", "Leading the World Astray"
Author/ Date	By Michael W. Chapman / February 28, 2020

In this chapter we looked at a number of mysteries from the Book of Revelation along with the correlation between the first five seals and the Olivet discourse from Matthew Chapter 24. We also showed that five of those seals have already been opened. In the next chapter, we are going to do a review of the Jewish feast days and investigate as to whether any of these days have been fulfilled. We will also look at which feast days are next in line for fulfillment.

Chapter Six
Understanding Revelation's Mysteries

Worksheet Questions for Chapter 6

1.   What is the dual threaded message to the seven churches in Asia Minor?

2.   In the last chapter we looked at five things that Jesus warned us to watch for. What is it that we should be watching for and how do these five warnings relate to the first five seals of Revelation?

3.   What is Revelation 6:6 telling us when it says "*a measure of wheat for a penny, and three measures of barley for a penny*"?

4.   After a seal from the Book of Revelation is opened, do the consequences of the opening of that seal cease once the next seal is opened?

5.   Is the Christian church being persecuted in the world today?

The Three Woes
A Guide To Understanding Revelation and End Time Prophecies

6. What are the Cosmic Signs?

7. How long are the *scorpion* locusts allowed to torment mankind?

8. What words indicated to us that the 5th trumpet angel has finished sounding, and where are those words located?

9. Where in Revelation does the 6th trumpet angel, the 2nd woe, begin to sound?

10. What timeframe does the 6th trumpet angel, the 2nd woe, correspond to?

11. What should we know about the time in Revelation 9:15?

12. What is the main focus of what is taking place during the 42 month time span of this 2nd woe?

Chapter Six
Understanding Revelation's Mysteries

13. What event marks the exact middle of the seven year tribulation period?

14. Who are the three personages that make up the Satanic Trinity in the 3rd woe?

15. Once the antichrist rises to power, how long will he retain his power?

16. The mark of the beast is really one of three things, what are they?

17. What does RFID stand for?

18. What happens at the end of the 42 month time span of the 3rd woe?

19. Who do you think the antichrist is?

The Three Woes
A Guide To Understanding Revelation and End Time Prophecies

20. What is the prophecy of St. Malachy?

21. Who do you think the false prophet is?

Chapter Seven
Fulfillment of the Feast Days

In this chapter we are going to look at the Jewish feast days to see how they might relate to Biblical history and to the prophetic future. Before we jump into the feast days, it would probably be beneficial to give everyone a basic understanding of the Jewish calendar, since it differs quite a bit from the Gregorian calendar that most of us are accustomed to using.

The Gregorian calendar is actually much more complicated than the Jewish calendar. The Gregorian calendar begins with January and has seven months with 31 days, four months with 30 days and one month with either 28 or 29 days, depending on leap year. Take Easter for example, the Gregorian calendar calculates it as the first Sunday following the first full moon following the spring equinox. This is why it fluctuates between March 22nd and the 25th of April.

The Jewish calendar begins with the month Tishrei and the calendar is mostly based on the lunar cycle which consists of 29.53 days. The first day of Tishrei is called Rosh Hashanah (New Year) and occurs sometime between early September and mid October on the Gregorian calendar. It fluctuates, just like Easter, because of the cycles of the moon. The Jewish calendar months typically alternate between 29 and 30 days. The Jewish calendar contains a month called Adar and every few years the Jewish calendar adds an additional month called Adar II to account for what we call leap year.

The Three Woes
A Guide To Understanding Revelation and End Time Prophecies

The Jewish Feast Days Ordained by God in Leviticus

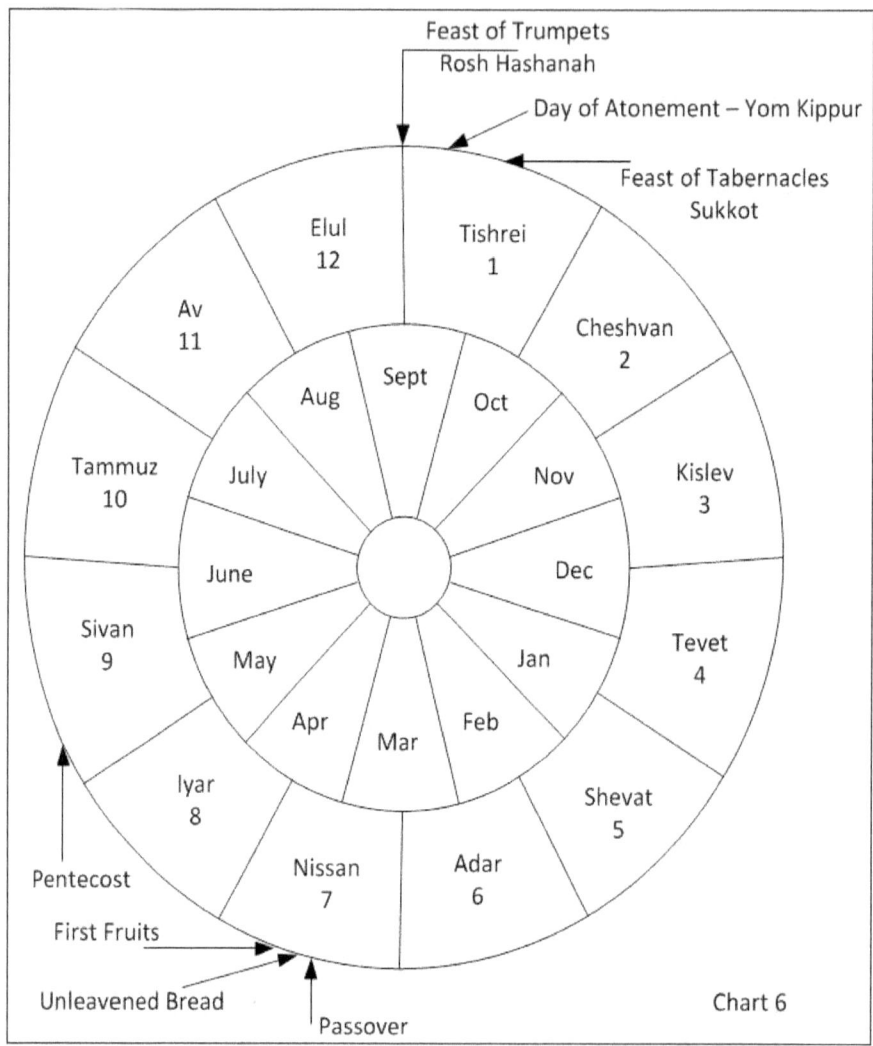

Chart 6

The following link is to an excellent site that shows both the Gregorian and Jewish calendars along with designated feast days.

https://www.chabad.org/calendar/view/month.asp?tdate=9/15/2020

Chapter Seven
Fulfillment of the Feast Days

Now that we have reviewed the Jewish calendar, we will turn our attention to the Jewish feast days. Since the Jewish people are one of the oldest people groups in the world, dating back several thousand years, it only stands to reason that the people would have added numerous feasts over the years, and that is exactly what they have done. But what we want to look at are the feasts that were commanded and ordained by God. The original feasts that were commanded by God are a total of seven and they are conveniently all located in Chapter 23 of Leviticus.

It would be beneficial to read the full chapter of Leviticus, but for the sake of brevity, we will not do that at this time. We will limit our discussion to the first two verses where God gives the command to keep these feast days and to the verses that define the name of the specified feast.

> *And the Lord spake unto Moses, saying, 2 Speak unto the children of Israel, and say unto them, Concerning the feasts of the Lord, which ye shall proclaim to be holy convocations, even these are my feasts.*
> **Leviticus 23:1-2 KJV**

Jewish Feast Day	Ordained by God in Leviticus
Passover	*In the fourteenth day of the first month at even is the Lord's passover.* **Leviticus 23:5 KJV**
Seder	*And on the fifteenth day of the same month is the feast of unleavened bread unto the Lord: seven days ye must eat unleavened bread.* **Leviticus 23:6 KJV**
Yom HaBikkurim	*Ye shall bring out of your habitations two wave loaves of two tenth deals: they shall be of fine flour; they shall be baken with leaven;*

	they are the firstfruits unto the Lord. **Leviticus 23:17 KJV**
Shavuot	*Even unto the morrow after the seventh sabbath shall ye number fifty days; and ye shall offer a new meat offering unto the Lord.* **Leviticus 23:16 KJV**
Rosh Hashanah	*Speak unto the children of Israel, saying, In the seventh month, in the first day of the month, shall ye have a sabbath, a memorial of blowing of trumpets, an holy convocation.* **Leviticus 23:24 KJV**
Yom Kippur	*Also on the tenth day of this seventh month there shall be a day of atonement: it shall be an holy convocation unto you; and ye shall afflict your souls, and offer an offering made by fire unto the Lord.* **Leviticus 23:27 KJV**
Sukkot	*Speak unto the children of Israel, saying, The fifteenth day of this seventh month shall be the feast of tabernacles for seven days unto the Lord.* **Leviticus 23:34 KJV**

What we see in Verses 1 & 2 of this 23rd Chapter of Leviticus is God's commandment to the people of Israel to observe these seven feasts. As we begin to look at the feasts, the first thing that catches our attention is that the Feast of Passover is to occur on the fourteenth day of the first month. As we were looking at the Jewish calendar system we saw that the first month of the Jewish calendar is Tishrei and it occurs during our fall months of September or October. So how can Passover that coincides with the Christian observance of Good Friday, the day of Christ's crucifixion, be defined as the first month? Passover is celebrated

Chapter Seven
Fulfillment of the Feast Days

on the 14th day of Nissan at the time of the full moon and Nissan is the seventh month in the Jewish calendar. So why does God specify the first month here? Good question. It is believed that it is called the first month here because Nissan was the first month following the Jewish exodus from Egypt. God wasn't referring to the first month in the calendar but the first month following the Exodus.

As we begin to look at these feasts, we need to remember that these feast days or holidays are not like our holidays. We declare our holidays, but God declared these holidays. The word holiday is actually two words, Holy and Day from which we created the word holyday or as we say it now, holiday. God gave the Jewish people these feast days and they had a historic significance, but they also had a prophetic significance. Their historical symbolisms were as feasts of remembrance, while their forward looking symbolisms pointed to the coming Messiah. Both of these symbolisms were originally directed to the Jewish people but when they rejected the Messiah, the forward looking symbolism became the hope and promise of the gentile church. Unfortunately, the Jewish people missed this forward looking revelation.

> *And he began to teach them, that the Son of man must suffer many things, and be rejected of the elders, and of the chief priests, and scribes, and be killed, and after three days rise again*
> **Mark 8:31 KJV**

Jewish Feast Day	Leviticus Equivalent	Christian New Testament Equivalent	Status
Passover	Feast of Passover	Christ's Death	**Fulfilled**
Seder	Feast of Unleavened Bread	Christ's Burial	**Fulfilled**
Yom HaBikkurim	Feast of First Fruits	Christ's Resurrection	**Fulfilled**
Shavuot	Festival of Weeks	Pentecost, Giving of the Holy Spirit	**Fulfilled**
Rosh Hashanah	Feast of Trumpets	Christ's Return to Rapture His Church	unfulfilled
Yom Kippur	Feast of Atonement	Christ's Return to Earth	unfulfilled
Sukkot	Feast of Tabernacles	Christ's 1,000 Year Millennial Reign	unfulfilled

The Passover - Christ's Death

So now that we have dealt with the issue of the first month, let's move on and focus on the purpose of the Passover feast. For the Jewish people, Passover was a festival celebrating their Exodus from Egypt. This celebration always occurs in the spring on Nissan 15. What the Jewish people did not seem to realize is that the feasts were all pointing symbolically to the coming promised Messiah. In other words, they were "prophetic in nature," each one pointing in a unique way to some aspect of the life and work of the promised Messiah, Jesus. This is confirmed by the disciple

Chapter Seven
Fulfillment of the Feast Days

Mark and also by Paul in the verses below. Mark is telling us about the nearness of the Passover feast and also of the Feast of Unleavened Bread and how the chief priests and scribes are planning to kill Jesus. Paul further confirms this as we look at the verse from Corinthians where he calls Christ our passover sacrifice. Jesus was crucified on the day of preparation for the Passover, at the same time that the lambs were being slaughtered for the Passover meal that evening.

> *After two days was the feast of the passover, and of unleavened bread: and the chief priests and the scribes sought how they might take him by craft, and put him to death.*
> **Mark 14:1 KJV**

> *Your glorying is not good. Know ye not that a little leaven leaveneth the whole lump? 7 Purge out therefore the old leaven, that ye may be a new lump, as ye are unleavened. For even Christ our passover is sacrificed for us:*
> **1 Corinthians 5:6-7 KJV**

> *The next day John seeth Jesus coming unto him, and saith, Behold the Lamb of God, which taketh away the sin of the world.*
> **John 1:29 KJV**

The Feast of Unleavened Bread - Christ's Burial

The Seder, the Feast of Unleavened Bread, is frequently confused with the Feast of the Passover. The Feast of the Passover is a 24 hour feast, while the Seder is a seven day feast that begins the day after the Passover feast. The Jewish people were commanded to use no leaven in their bread. It takes time for the leavened bread to rise and the Jewish people needed to be prepared to leave Egypt as soon as Moses gave the command. So the order was given prior to the Exodus, to remove the leaven, a type of sin, and be prepared to leave Egypt.

Jesus, our Messiah, lived a sinless life, a life without leaven, making Him the perfect sacrifice for our sins. When he was crucified and died, fulfilling the Passover feast, the Jews asked Pilate, that Jesus and the other men's legs might be broken, that He might be taken away and buried in preparation for the Sabbath. Christ was already dead so His legs were not broken. Christ was then placed in the borrowed tomb, where He laid three days fulfilling the feast of Unleavened Bread and was resurrected Sunday morning.

> *The Jews therefore, because it was the preparation, that the bodies should not remain upon the cross on the sabbath day, (for that sabbath day was an high day,) besought Pilate that their legs might be broken, and that they might be taken away. 32 Then came the soldiers, and brake the legs of the first, and of the other which was crucified with him. 33 But when they came to Jesus, and saw that he was dead already, they brake not his legs: 34 But one of the soldiers with a spear pierced his side, and forthwith came there out blood and water. 35 And he that saw it bare record, and his record is true: and he knoweth that he saith true, that ye might believe. 36 For these things were done, that the scripture should be fulfilled, A bone of him shall not be broken. 37 And again another scripture saith, They shall look on him whom they pierced.*
> **John 19:31-37 KJV**

Chapter Seven
Fulfillment of the Feast Days

The Feast of First Fruits - Christ's Resurrection

The Feast of First Fruits or Yom HaBikkurim is not widely celebrated in Judaism. In fact, most Jewish people would probably associate first fruits with Shavuot, or Pentecost if you asked them about it, but it is a feast day specified by God in the Old Testament. For Christians, Jesus is called the first fruits of those who will rise from the dead. Jesus rose from the grave early in the morning three days and nights after His crucifixion. The Resurrection of Jesus came on the first day of the week, that day happened to be the 17th of Nissan, right on the Feast of First Fruits. Today, the Christian celebration of the risen Christ is Easter. For the Christian, the Feast of First Fruits is probably the most important of all these feasts. Without Easter and the risen Christ we would have no hope of our resurrection one day.

> *But now is Christ risen from the dead, and become the firstfruits of them that slept. 21 For since by man came death, by man came also the resurrection of the dead. 22 For as in Adam all die, even so in Christ shall all be made alive. 23 But every man in his own order: Christ the firstfruits; afterward they that are Christ's at his coming.*
> **1 Corinthians 15:20-23 KJV**

> *And God hath both raised up the Lord, and will also raise up us by his own power.*
> **1 Corinthians 6:14 KJV**

Passion Week

The above three Jewish feast celebrations are known in the Christian religion as the Passion Week. Jesus was crucified on Passover, answering to the Blood of the Lamb. He was buried on Unleavened Bread and He was raised on First Fruits, as a demonstration of the future resurrection of the church. That wasn't the end of the Lord's ministry on earth, He continued by fulfilling His promise regarding the sending of the Holy Spirit. The fourth feast, Pentecost, occurred 50 days later, on that very day, the Holy Spirit fell upon the Pentecost festivities in the house where they were gathered.

The Feast of Weeks - Giving of the Holy Spirit

Shavuot is a Hebrew word meaning weeks. The Greek word for Shavuot is Pentecost, meaning fiftieth. It occurs seven weeks following Passover. In Judaism, the period of counting the days from Passover until Shavuot is called Counting the Omer. The Torah mandates the seven week Counting of the Omer, beginning on the second day of Passover. In Luke Chapter 24 we see where Jesus told His disciples to tarry until His Father sent the promise, the Holy Spirit. Then in the Book of Acts, we see the day called Pentecost (50 days) where the Christian believers were all filled with the Holy Ghost.

> *And, behold, I send the promise of my Father upon you: but tarry ye in the city of Jerusalem, until ye be endued with power from on high.*
> **Luke 24:49 KJV**

> *And when the day of Pentecost was fully come, they were all with one accord in one place. 2 And suddenly there came a sound from heaven as of a rushing mighty wind, and it filled all the house where they were sitting. 3 And there appeared unto them cloven tongues like as of fire, and it sat upon each of them. 4 And they were all filled*

Chapter Seven
Fulfillment of the Feast Days

with the Holy Ghost, and began to speak with other tongues, as the Spirit gave them utterance.
Acts 2:1-4 KJV

The Feast of Weeks and the giving of the Holy Spirit concluded the Messianic fulfillment of the first four spring feasts that God ordained in the Book of Leviticus. There are three feasts remaining that have not yet been fulfilled. The remaining feasts are the fall feasts and all three occur within a two week time frame on the Hebrew calendar much like the first three spring feasts. These feasts are: (1) the Feast of Trumpets where Christ will return in the air, to rapture His church, (2) the Feast of Atonement where Christ will return to earth and to the Battle of Armageddon at the end of the great tribulation, and (3) the Feast of Tabernacles where Christ establishes His 1,000 year Millennial reign.

Because Jesus literally fulfilled the first four feasts, and did so on the actual feast days, it seems safe to assume that the last three feast days will be fulfilled in a somewhat similar manner. That is to say, the fulfillment of the actual feasts will be fulfilled like they were 2,000 years ago, but these feasts will not be fulfilled in a two week span of actual time like the feasts occur on the Jewish calendar. The Messianic fulfillment of the Feast of Trumpets will occur on its feast day and then the Messianic fulfillment of the Feast of Atonement will most likely occur on its feast day eight years later, symbolic of its being eight days later on the calendar. The Messianic fulfillment of the Feast of Tabernacles will probably occur in the same year as the Feast of Atonement.

The Feast of Trumpets - Christ Raptures His Church

The first of the fall feasts is the Feast of Trumpets or as the Jews call it, Rosh Hashanah, the beginning of the year, or the Jewish

New Year. It is a sacred occasion that is commemorated with loud blasts on a shofar, the ram's horn. The Jewish themes of the festival are: (1) repentance, (2) preparation for the day of Divine judgment, and (3) prayer for a fruitful year. It is a two-day festival that falls on Tishrei 1 through 2 of the Jewish calendar.

For the Christian, Rosh Hashanah points to the Rapture of the Christian church, when the Messiah will appear in the heavens as a Bridegroom coming for His bride, the Church. The Rapture is always associated in Scripture with the blowing of a loud trumpet, the shofar. During the Feast of Trumpets, the trumpet is blown a total of 100 times, with the final horn blast lasting much longer than the first 99 blasts.

> *In a moment, in the twinkling of an eye, at the last trump: for the trumpet shall sound, and the dead shall be raised incorruptible, and we shall be changed.*
> **1 Corinthians 15:52 KJV**

> *And he shall send his angels with a great sound of a trumpet, and they shall gather together his elect from the four winds, from one end of heaven to the other*
> **Matthew 24:31 KJV**

The Feast of Atonement - Christ's Return to Earth

The Feast of Atonement or Yom Kippur occurs eight days after Rosh Hashanah. Remember, the Feast of Atonement will herald Jesus' second coming to earth and will probably occur eight years after the rapture of the church. For the Jewish people it is a time of atonement, to pray for forgiveness for sins against man and God. It is a time to enumerate one's misdeeds and contemplate one's faults, so that the individual may be cleansed of sins.

Chapter Seven
Fulfillment of the Feast Days

As we look at this Day of Atonement, not as a yearly practice, but as the Messianic fulfillment and final Day of Atonement, it seems to have a dual meaning. For the Jewish people, or nation as a whole, it seems to be the time of God's acceptance of their repentance. Just as God turned to the gentiles and away from the Jewish nation 2,000 years ago when Israel rejected God's Messiah, this will mark the point in time where God will once again turn His attention back to the nation of Israel and away from the gentiles.

It seems, for the gentiles that it may become more a time of judgment. Within the gentile church as a whole, there has been a great falling away prior to this Day of Atonement, even prior to the seven years of tribulation that the world will shortly experience. The time for the gentiles of the world to come to Jesus with a heart of repentance is now, not on this Day of Atonement. This will be the day that the bride of Christ, His church, will return to earth with Christ, when He comes the second time at the Battle of Armageddon.

> *And I will pour upon the house of David, and upon the inhabitants of Jerusalem, the spirit of grace and of supplications: and they shall look upon me whom they have pierced, and they shall mourn for him, as one mourneth for his only son, and shall be in bitterness for him, as one that is in bitterness for his firstborn.*
> **Zechariah 12:10 KJV**

> *For I would not, brethren, that ye should be ignorant of this mystery, lest ye should be wise in your own conceits; that blindness in part is happened to Israel, until the fulness of the Gentiles be come in. 26 And so all Israel shall be saved: as it is written, There shall come out of Sion the Deliverer,*

> *and shall turn away ungodliness from Jacob: 27 For this is my covenant unto them, when I shall take away their sins.*
> **Romans 11:25-27 KJV**

> *And he gathered them together into a place called in the Hebrew tongue Armageddon.*
> **Revelation 16:16 KJV**

The Feast of the Tabernacles - Christ's Millennial Reign

The Feast of Tabernacles or Sukkot begins five days after Yom Kippur. The name Chag HaSukkot refers to the temporary dwellings God made to shelter the Jewish people on their exodus out of Egypt. It symbolically points to the Lord's promise that He will once again tabernacle with His people when He returns to reign over all the world for a thousand years from Jerusalem. Sukkot commonly goes by the name "The Season of Our Joy" within the Jewish community, and it will certainly be a season of joy when He is ruling over them for a thousand years. The Feast of Tabernacles is an annual reminder to the Jewish people that God is their Great Shepherd who has chosen to tabernacle among them, to protect and bless them wherever they wander. For the raptured church, it will be a blessed time as well as for the raptured saints, both those who died in Christ and those who were caught away in the air, will reign with Christ during His thousand year reign on earth.

> *And it shall come to pass, that every one that is left of all the nations which came against Jerusalem shall even go up from year to year to worship the King, the Lord of hosts, and to keep the feast of tabernacles.*
> **Zechariah 14:16 KJV**

Chapter Seven
Fulfillment of the Feast Days

And I saw an angel come down from heaven, having the key of the bottomless pit and a great chain in his hand. 2 And he laid hold on the dragon, that old serpent, which is the Devil, and Satan, and bound him a thousand years, 3 And cast him into the bottomless pit, and shut him up, and set a seal upon him, that he should deceive the nations no more, till the thousand years should be fulfilled: and after that he must be loosed a little season. 4 And I saw thrones, and they sat upon them, and judgment was given unto them: and I saw the souls of them that were beheaded for the witness of Jesus, and for the word of God, and which had not worshipped the beast, neither his image, neither had received his mark upon their foreheads, or in their hands; and they lived and reigned with Christ a thousand years.
Revelation 20:1-4 KJV

No Man Knows the Day Nor Hour

Some may be saying about now, "There's another prediction on when Christ will return, and we all know that the scripture says that, no man knows the day nor the hour." That is entirely true, no one knows the day nor the hour, but what is the whole truth of what the Bible teaches us about knowing the times?

Watch therefore, for ye know neither the day nor the hour wherein the Son of man cometh.
Matthew 25:13 KJV

Let's start by looking at a couple of verses in Acts and also three verses in First Thessalonians. Both of these scripture references have something to say about knowing the 'times and seasons'. In

Acts, Jesus is quoted as saying that it is not for the disciples to know the "times or the seasons," while in Thessalonians Paul tells the Thessalonians that they already know the "times and the seasons." So, is Paul wrong since the word of Jesus would certainly override the word of Paul? Not at all. Paul and Jesus are talking about two different subjects. The subject of these verses is not "times and seasons."

> *When they therefore were come together, they asked of him, saying, Lord, wilt thou at this time restore again the kingdom to Israel? 7 And he said unto them, It is not for you to know the times or the seasons, which the Father hath put in his own power.*
> **Acts 1:6-7 KJV**

> *But of the times and the seasons, brethren, ye have no need that I write unto you. 2 For yourselves know perfectly that the day of the Lord so cometh as a thief in the night. 3 For when they shall say, Peace and safety; then sudden destruction cometh upon them, as travail upon a woman with child; and they shall not escape.*
> **1 Thessalonians 5:1-3 KJV**

In Acts, the real subject is "will Jesus at this time restore the kingdom to Israel," and the subject in Thessalonians is "the day of the Lord," or in other words, the return of Christ to rapture His church. Most of us would agree that these are definitely two different subjects occurring at two different points in time. Jesus is telling His audience that they don't need to know when the kingdom will be restored, while Paul is telling his audience that they already do know the signs of Christ's return. We can see further proof of this by looking at Luke 12:56, where Jesus is quoted as calling the people hypocrites because they can discern the weather, but they claim they can't discern the time.

Chapter Seven
Fulfillment of the Feast Days

Ye hypocrites, ye can discern the face of the sky and of the earth; but how is it that ye do not discern this time?
Luke 12:56 KJV

Discerning the Time and Season

Paul goes on to tell the Thessalonians that "the Lord will come like a thief in the night." That phrase doesn't mean much to people today, but to the Thessalonians who would have been familiar with the Jewish temple and traditions, it meant a lot. God had commanded that the fire upon the temple altar was to never go out. Levite priests would be assigned to tend the temple fire all day and all night to keep the altar fire burning. To ensure that the fire did not go out by night, the captain or chief priest would come through the temple at night making sure the fire was burning and the priest was awake. The priest who was on duty never knew when the captain would come to check on the tending priest. The captain was a type of Christ, the Messiah.

> *Command Aaron and his sons, saying, This is the law of the burnt offering: It is the burnt offering, because of the burning upon the altar all night unto the morning, and the fire of the altar shall be burning in it.*
> **Leviticus 6:9 KJV**

> *The fire shall ever be burning upon the altar; it shall never go out.*
> **Leviticus 6:13 KJV**

If the chief priest ever found the tending priest asleep, the chief priest would take his torch and set the garments of the priest who had fallen asleep on fire. When the unwatchful priest would awake and find his garments on fire he would run out of the temple stripping off his fiery garments. The priest would then run down the street naked with his shame exposed. This short history lesson from the days of the temple brings to life the real meaning and understanding of the following verse from Revelation.

> *Behold, I come as a thief. Blessed is he that watcheth, and keepeth his garments, lest he walk naked, and they see his shame.*
> **Revelation 16:15 KJV**

Just as the priest tending the fire through the night did not know at what hour the captain would come, so we do not know the hour. But God has told us that we should and will be able to discern the times and the season of Christ's coming. The priest knew the captain would come at sometime during the night but he didn't know at what hour he would come. The coming of our Lord will be much like this. We won't know the day nor the hour but we are to discern the time and season. As we look around us, we are definitely in that time and season, but as to the day and the hour, we don't know.

Think about the world, when Christ returns to rapture His church, He will circumvent the earth in the twinkling of an eye collecting His saints. A twinkle is less time than it takes to blink your eye. For some His return will be today but for others it will be yesterday or tomorrow depending on which side of the International Date Line you are living on. For some He will come at midnight but for others He will come at noon day. Think about the New Year celebration in the western hemisphere, it can be early afternoon on New Year's Eve and people in America are watching Sidney, Australia ring in the New Year. Our earth is divided into twenty four time zones, and for each one the rapture will occur at a different hour. As the Word tells us, we will not know the day nor the hour, but we can know the time and the season.

Chapter Seven
Fulfillment of the Feast Days

Behold, I shew you a mystery; We shall not all sleep, but we shall all be changed, 52 In a moment, in the twinkling of an eye, at the last trump: for the trumpet shall sound, and the dead shall be raised incorruptible, and we shall be changed.
1 Corinthians 15:51-52 KJV

We need to be awake and be watchful, ready for Christ's appearing, lest we fall asleep and He set our garments on fire and the shame of our nakedness be exposed. In the next chapter, we are going to explore in more depth, the greatest prophecy of all, the promised return of Jesus Christ.

The Three Woes
A Guide To Understanding Revelation and End Time Prophecies

Worksheet Questions for Chapter 7

1. What is the Jewish calendar based on?

2. What do the Jewish people call the 1st day of the 1st month (our New Years day)?

3. In Leviticus 23:5 God speaks about Passover, which equates to our Good Friday, as being the 14th day of the 1st month. How can Passover be in the spring of the year if God said it is in the 1st month and we just defined that the Jewish New Year occurs in the fall?

4. What are the first four spring feast days that God ordained in Leviticus 23?

5. Which of these four feasts have been fulfilled?

Chapter Seven
Fulfillment of the Feast Days

6. What are the next three feasts form Leviticus that have not yet been fulfilled?

7. What are the Jewish celebration themes for Rosh Hashanah, the feast of trumpets?

8. What do you think about the scripture in Matthew where it says "ye know neither the day nor the hour"?

Chapter Eight
The Greatest Prophecy of All, The Return of Jesus Christ

In this chapter we are going to look at the prophecies concerning the return of Jesus. They are very important because all the hopes of the Christian church and even of the whole world are dependent on the fulfillment of this prophecy. But before we look at the prophecies of His return, we should probably review just why the prophecy of His return is so very important.

Why is the Fulfillment of this Prophecy so Necessary?

The answer to that question goes back approximately six thousand years. Adam and Eve were living a sinless life in the Garden of Eden where God had created them to fellowship with Him. The garden and the whole earth were given to them by God. They had dominion over the earth. The earth and the Garden of Eden was theirs to enjoy and to care for. Only one item was kept from them, the fruit from the "tree of the knowledge of good and evil." It was a very simple command to see if they would be obedient to God or disobedient.

> *And God said, Let us make man in our image, after our likeness: and let them have dominion over the fish of the sea, and over the fowl of the air, and over the cattle, and over all the earth, and over every creeping thing that creepeth upon the earth.*
> **Genesis 1:26 KJV**

> *And the Lord God planted a garden eastward in Eden; and there he put the man whom he had formed. 9 And out of the ground made the Lord God to grow every tree that is*

> *pleasant to the sight, and good for food; the tree of life also in the midst of the garden, and the tree of knowledge of good and evil.*
> **Genesis 2:8-9 KJV**

> *And the Lord God took the man, and put him into the garden of Eden to dress it and to keep it. 16 And the Lord God commanded the man, saying, Of every tree of the garden thou mayest freely eat: 17 But of the tree of the knowledge of good and evil, thou shalt not eat of it: for in the day that thou eatest thereof thou shalt surely die.*
> **Genesis 2:15-17 KJV**

Before we continue, notice that Adam and Eve had free access to every tree in the garden. All the trees were there for them to partake of and enjoy. There was only one tree that God had set aside and forbade them to eat from. We are not told how long Adam and Eve lived in the garden before they ate of the forbidden tree and were cast out of the garden, but it was long enough for them to grow accustomed to meeting with God and to walk with Him in the cool of the day.

All was fine until one day the serpent came along and tempted Eve. The serpent cunningly and deceitfully tempted Eve to eat of the forbidden fruit from the "tree of the knowledge of good and evil." Once Eve had eaten of the fruit, she gave it to Adam and he ate as well. Two things happened that day: (1) Adam and Eve lost their innocence when they chose to disobey God, and (2) Adam yielded up his dominion over the earth. Satan claimed temporary dominion over the earth and Adam and Eve chose death over life. Since that day, all mankind has eventually died with the exception of two that God, in His wisdom and authority, chose to deliver for some other purpose.

Chapter Eight
The Greatest Prophecy of All, The Return of Jesus Christ

Now the serpent was more subtil than any beast of the field which the Lord God had made. And he said unto the woman, Yea, hath God said, Ye shall not eat of every tree of the garden?
Genesis 3:1 KJV

And when the woman saw that the tree was good for food, and that it was pleasant to the eyes, and a tree to be desired to make one wise, she took of the fruit thereof, and did eat, and gave also unto her husband with her; and he did eat.
Genesis 3:6 KJV

And the Lord God called unto Adam, and said unto him, Where art thou?
Genesis 3:9 KJV

And unto Adam he said, Because thou hast hearkened unto the voice of thy wife, and hast eaten of the tree, of which I commanded thee, saying, Thou shalt not eat of it: cursed is the ground for thy sake; in sorrow shalt thou eat of it all the days of thy life;
Genesis 3:17 KJV

In the sweat of thy face shalt thou eat bread, till thou return unto the ground; for out of it wast thou taken: for dust thou art, and unto dust shalt thou return.
Genesis 3:19 KJV

So why would we say that Adam and Eve chose death over life? As we look at the above scriptures, we are told in Genesis 2:9 that every tree that is pleasant and good to eat was in the Garden of Eden. God also specifically names two trees in the garden. They are: (1) the "tree of life," and (2) the "tree of the knowledge of good and evil." The names of both of these trees are self descriptive. The one offered life and the other offered knowledge and death. Adam and Eve chose to eat from the "tree of knowledge of good and evil."

> *Wherefore, as by one man sin entered into the world, and death by sin; and so death passed upon all men, for that all have sinned:*
> **Romans 5:12 KJV**

While we can't know for sure, it is certainly implied that Adam and Eve never ate from the "tree of life." We can say that, because, Genesis 3:22 implies that Adam and Eve could still live forever if they were to eat from the "tree of life," even though they had already disobeyed God and eaten from the "tree of the knowledge of good and evil." That implication certainly would lead one to believe that Adam and Eve had the option to choose to eat from either of those two trees while they were in the garden and they chose to eat from the "tree of knowledge of good and evil" which lead to death, never availing themselves of the "tree of life."

> *And the Lord God said, Behold, the man is become as one of us, to know good and evil: and now, lest he put forth his hand, and take also of the tree of life, and eat, and live for ever:* 23 *Therefore the Lord God sent him forth from the garden of Eden, to till the ground from whence he was taken.*
> **Genesis 3:22-23 KJV**

When Adam and Eve sinned against God by partaking of the forbidden fruit, not only did they sin personally, but through them, the sin nature and the knowledge of good and evil entered the human race. So you might say, how do we know that? The

Chapter Eight
The Greatest Prophecy of All, The Return of Jesus Christ

answer to that is pretty straight forward. Before their sin and personal disobedience, Adam and Eve had no concept of their nakedness or of any good or evil, but following their sin and the loss of their innocence, they did have that knowledge.

As we look at their offspring Cain and Abel, it isn't long before we see the sin nature, inherited through their parents, expressing itself when Cain murders Abel in a jealous rage. The jealous rage occurred when Abel's offering to God was accepted and Cain's offering was rejected. Without the sin nature, Cain and Abel would have likewise been without the knowledge of good and evil, but they weren't.

Some may argue that this sin nature could not be inherited in this manner. If that was the case, then where did Cain and Abel get their knowledge of good and evil? Their parents were cast out of the Garden of Eden and no longer had access to the "tree of knowledge of good and evil." So Cain and Abel had to inherit the knowledge just as they inherited the sin nature. Cain and Abel inherited the sin nature, just as we inherit all our other traits from our parents. A couple with a sinful human nature can't expect to have a child without that same sinful human nature. Do we expect an Oriental couple to have a child with European traits, or a European couple to have a child with Oriental trails? Certainly not! It simply can't happen and so it is with all mankind. Parents with a sinful nature will produce children with the same sinful nature.

We see further evidence of the sinful fall of man in Chapter 6 of Genesis where God looks upon His creation of man and regrets that He ever created Him. God proclaims that mankind is so wicked that their every imagination and thought is only evil continually. God says that He repented that He ever made man and decides to destroy all flesh except for the eight members of

Noah's family. This story stifles the modern day concept that God is all love and mankind can do whatever he chooses because God will always be ready to accept us just as we are. God didn't accept the sin of the ancient world and God won't accept the sin of the modern world. Judgment is coming.

> *And God saw that the wickedness of man was great in the earth, and that every imagination of the thoughts of his heart was only evil continually. 6 And it repented the Lord that he had made man on the earth, and it grieved him at his heart.*
> **Genesis 6:5-6 KJV**

> *And, behold, I, even I, do bring a flood of waters upon the earth, to destroy all flesh, wherein is the breath of life, from under heaven; and every thing that is in the earth shall die.*
> **Genesis 6:17 KJV**

As we said earlier, God is love, but He is also just. We can even see His love in this story of the flood and His saving of Noah's family. It is easy to see the justice of God, where God used a flood to destroy all mankind, with the exception of Noah's family. But, it is easy to miss the love of God, where God waited patiently on Noah and his family to build the ark before carrying out His prescribed justice. We are not told specifically how long it took Noah and his family to build the ark, but estimates put it somewhere between one hundred years and one hundred and twenty years. God patiently waited and withheld His justice and judgment for many years while Noah was building the ark.

Chapter Eight
The Greatest Prophecy of All, The Return of Jesus Christ

> *But Noah found grace in the eyes of the Lord. 9 These are the generations of Noah: Noah was a just man and perfect in his generations, and Noah walked with God.*
> **Genesis 6:8-9 KJV**

Just as we are not told how long it took Noah and his family to build the ark, we are also not told about Noah's potential contacts with other people in the world during the years he was building the ark. One might assume that onlookers, watching Noah spend years building the ark, probably scoffed and laughed thinking it to be a great waste of time. Just as many people scoff and laugh at Christians today thinking they are wasting their time serving a God who they say "doesn't exist and isn't returning." The scripture even tells us that "as in the days of Noe (Noah) so shall also the coming of the Son of man be."

> *But as the days of Noe were, so shall also the coming of the Son of man be.*
> **Matthew 24:37 KJV**

The Need for a Savior

So what we see from the time of Adam and Eve until the time of Noah is mankind's spiritual decline and desperate need for a Savior. We and all mankind need a Savior to forgive us of all our personal sins as well as to deliver us from the sin nature. The great news is, God had a plan from the very beginning when He created Adam, to provide us with a Savior and to deliver us. That plan was fulfilled approximately four thousand years after Adam and Eve partook of the forbidden tree. The fulfillment came when a young virgin girl named Mary conceived a child of the Holy Spirit and gave birth to that child calling Him Jesus.

> *Therefore the Lord himself shall give you a sign; Behold, a virgin shall conceive, and bear a son, and shall call his name Immanuel.*
> **Isaiah 7:14 KJV**

> *Now the birth of Jesus Christ was on this wise: When as his mother Mary was espoused to Joseph, before they came together, she was found with child of the Holy Ghost.*
> **Matthew 1:18 KJV**

We need a Savior because we need to be forgiven of our sins and made holy. We can't do it for ourselves and no one else who is sinful, or has ever sinned, can do it for us. For God's justice to be satisfied we must either accept the punishment ourselves or our debt and punishment must be paid by someone who is without sin and someone who has never sinned. God provided that someone. Jesus is the only one who can claim that title of being sinless and without the sin nature.

> *For the wages of sin is death; but the gift of God is eternal life through Jesus Christ our Lord.*
> **Romans 6:23 KJV**

> *For God so loved the world, that he gave his only begotten Son, that whosoever believeth in him should not perish, but have everlasting life.*
> **John 3:16 KJV**

Jesus alone can come forward and take our place. He is the only One who has never sinned and the only One who did not inherit the sin nature from Adam. Jesus received His humanity from Mary, His mother, and He received His sinless nature from the Holy Spirit. Jesus, through the shedding of His blood, makes

Chapter Eight
The Greatest Prophecy of All, The Return of Jesus Christ

atonement for our sins and makes us completely new creatures in Him.

> *For he hath made him to be sin for us, who knew no sin; that we might be made the righteousness of God in him.*
> **2 Corinthians 5:21 KJV**

> *Follow peace with all men, and holiness, without which no man shall see the Lord:*
> **Hebrews 12:14 KJV**

> *By the which will we are sanctified through the offering of the body of Jesus Christ once for all.*
> **Hebrews 10:10 KJV**

The Blood Sacrifice

Through Jesus and the shedding of His blood, we can obtain forgiveness of sins and have that sin nature taken from us. It is from no acts or works that we can do but only through the sinless shed blood of Jesus. The only part that we, as mere humans, play in this redemptive process is to ask for God's forgiveness with a repentant heart and attitude, and accept the free gift of pardon that God provided through His redemptive plan. Lost and fallen mankind needed a Savior to provide a means for man to escape God's judgment and that Savior is the God-Man Jesus Christ.

> *For the life of the flesh is in the blood: and I have given it to you upon the altar to make an atonement for your souls: for it is the blood that maketh an atonement for the soul.*
> **Leviticus 17:11 KJV**

So why is the shedding of blood necessary? The answer to that goes back to Adam and Eve as well. After they sinned by eating the forbidden fruit, God killed innocent sinless animals to cover their nakedness. The shedding of the animal's blood was a temporary atonement for sin. In this case, the animal introduced the concept of an innocent party taking the punishment for a guilty party. The innocent animal was a provisional sacrifice for sin pointing to the permanent sacrifice that Jesus would one day provide. This is why Jesus had to not only live a sinless life but He also had to be free of the sin nature that mankind inherited from Adam.

> *Then shall he kill the goat of the sin offering, that is for the people, and bring his blood within the vail...*
> **Leviticus 16:15 KJV.**

> *One kid of the goats for a sin offering; beside the sin offering of atonement...*
> **Numbers 29:11 KJV**

Jesus did for mankind what no animal could ever do. No animal could ever really atone for man's sins. The animal sacrifices of the Old Testament were only temporary placeholders until a satisfactory and fully qualified sacrifice could be provided. Since it was a man who committed the sin, the only sacrifice that would satisfy God's justice was another man. The problem was that no mere man could ever qualify because all were unworthy due to the sin nature inherited from Adam.

God, in His infinite love, offered His own Son to be born of a virgin. Jesus did not inherit the sin nature from Adam but instead Jesus inherited God's Holy nature that enabled Him to live a sinless life. Because of Jesus' Holy nature and sinless life, He was

Chapter Eight
The Greatest Prophecy of All, The Return of Jesus Christ

qualified to be that perfect sacrifice to atone for mankind's sinful acts once and for all.

We Need a Savior to Escape the Second Death

Earlier we talked about Adam and Eve dying when they ate the forbidden fruit. Some might say, they didn't die, they lived to be over nine hundred years old. That is true, Adam did live to be nine hundred and thirty years old. But, there is more than one type of death. There are in fact three types of death: (1) physical death, (2) spiritual death, and (3) eternal death.

When Adam and Eve disobeyed God, they died spiritually. It wasn't the fruit that caused the death but the act of disobedience. When God created Adam and Eve, they were holy beings created in God's image. Through that act of disobedience they lost their holy nature and it was replaced with the sinful nature that all mankind has inherited ever since. That sinful nature is spiritual death. Adam and Eve, like the rest of mankind, both eventually died a physical death as well.

So where does eternal death come in? When God created man He created him in His own image. We are eternal beings like God is eternal. Our being, our essence, is our spirit. Our bodies are formed from the dust of the earth. When God breathed into man the breath of life, He was breathing our spirit, our essence, into the physical body that was created from the dust of the earth. This merging of the body and spirit creates what is called a living soul.

> *So God created man in his own image, in the image of God created he him; male and female created he them.*
> **Genesis 1:27 KJV**

The Three Woes
A Guide To Understanding Revelation and End Time Prophecies

> *And the Lord God formed man of the dust of the ground, and breathed into his nostrils the breath of life; and man became a living soul*
> **Genesis 2:7 KJV**

Notice the order of creation in the verses above. In Genesis 1:27, God created man the spirit. Then in Genesis 2:7, God created the physical man from the dust. Next, God breathed the breath of life, man's spirit, into the nostrils, of the physical body. This is when man became a living soul. When a man's physical body dies his spirit or essence leaves the body but that spirit does not die, it is eternal. We see the proof of this below in the verse from the Book of James.

> *For as the body without the spirit is dead, so faith without works is dead also.*
> **James 2:26 KJV**

As we examine the verse from James, it is very important to note that the body without the spirit is dead, but it doesn't say that the spirit without the body is dead. When the body dies and the spirit leaves the body, that spirit would be called a disembodied spirit. It still exists only without physical form. The scripture tells us that the spirit of man returns to God when the physical body dies. That spirit of the man will still retain all the memories, all the feelings and all the emotions that the man had while alive in the body. To understand this, read the story about Lazarus and the rich man, as told by Jesus in Luke Chapter 16 below.

> *Then shall the dust return to the earth as it was: and the spirit shall return unto God who gave it.*
> **Ecclesiastes 12:7 KJV**

Chapter Eight
The Greatest Prophecy of All, The Return of Jesus Christ

There was a certain rich man, which was clothed in purple and fine linen, and fared sumptuously every day: 20 And there was a certain beggar named Lazarus, which was laid at his gate, full of sores, 21 And desiring to be fed with the crumbs which fell from the rich man's table: moreover the dogs came and licked his sores. 22 And it came to pass, that the beggar died, and was carried by the angels into Abraham's bosom: the rich man also died, and was buried; 23 And in hell he lift up his eyes, being in torments, and seeth Abraham afar off, and Lazarus in his bosom. 24 And he cried and said, Father Abraham, have mercy on me, and send Lazarus, that he may dip the tip of his finger in water, and cool my tongue; for I am tormented in this flame. 25 But Abraham said, Son, remember that thou in thy lifetime receivedst thy good things, and likewise Lazarus evil things: but now he is comforted, and thou art tormented. 26 And beside all this, between us and you there is a great gulf fixed: so that they which would pass from hence to you cannot; neither can they pass to us, that would come from thence. 27 Then he said, I pray thee therefore, father, that thou wouldest send him to my father's house: 28 For I have five brethren; that he may testify unto them, lest they also come into this place of torment. 29 Abraham saith unto him, They have Moses and the prophets; let them hear them. 30 And he said, Nay, father Abraham: but if one went unto them from the dead, they will repent. 31 And he said unto him, If they hear not Moses and the prophets, neither will they be persuaded, though one rose from the dead.

Luke 16:19-31 KJV

This torment that the rich man described is the second death. If we fail to avail ourselves of the provision provided by Jesus' shed blood on the cross, then we face the second death and will suffer the punishment for our sins ourselves, just like the rich man. If we give our lives to Jesus, confessing and repenting of our sins, then we will be comforted like Lazarus. We will be comforted in Abraham's bosom just like Lazarus until Jesus returns.

> *He that hath an ear, let him hear what the Spirit saith unto the churches; He that overcometh shall not be hurt of the second death.*
> **Revelation 2:11 KJV**

> *And death and hell were cast into the lake of fire. This is the second death.*
> **Revelation 20:14 KJV**

As we started this chapter, we said the return of Jesus was the hope of the Christian church and even the hope for the world. There are many wonderful promises associated with the return of Jesus and one of those promises, to those that live for Christ, is that of a new body. Many old time Christians would sing a song called *"Mansion Over the Hilltop."* That mansion is most likely the Christian's new glorified body. We know from Corinthians that those in Christ will receive a spiritual body and Peter gives us a picture of just what that spiritual body will be like. It will be incorruptible, undefiled and it will never fade away.

> *It is sown a natural body; it is raised a spiritual body. There is a natural body, and there is a spiritual body.*
> **1 Corinthians 15:44 KJV**

> *To an inheritance incorruptible, and undefiled, and that fadeth not away, reserved in heaven for you, 5 Who are kept by the power of God through faith unto salvation ready to be revealed in the last time.*
> **1 Peter 1:4-5 KJV**

Chapter Eight
The Greatest Prophecy of All, The Return of Jesus Christ

The Christian's confidence in receiving this glorified body is the empty tomb of Jesus. He was crucified on the cross and buried but, through the power of God, He rose on the third day. This was testified to and reported by hundreds of people as first hand observers. Those who have died in Christ and those who are alive and remain are eagerly awaiting Christ's return. He will soon return to gather the dead in Christ and to also catch away those who are alive.

> *Knowing that Christ being raised from the dead dieth no more; death hath no more dominion over him.*
> **Romans 6:9 KJV**

When He does return to catch away His church, He will not step foot on the earth, but about eight years later, He will return physically to the earth and establish His thousand year Millennial reign.

> *For unto us a child is born, unto us a son is given: and the government shall be upon his shoulder: and his name shall be called Wonderful, Counsellor, The mighty God, The everlasting Father, The Prince of Peace.*
> **Isaiah 9:6 KJV**

> *Blessed and holy is he that hath part in the first resurrection: on such the second death hath no power, but they shall be priests of God and of Christ, and shall reign with him a thousand years.*
> **Revelation 20:6 KJV**

For all those who are covered by the blood of Jesus, they will reign with Christ on earth for the thousand years. For all those who are not covered by the blood of Jesus, they will wait with the rich man to have their part in the lake of fire.

> *But the fearful, and unbelieving, and the abominable, and murderers, and whoremongers, and sorcerers, and idolaters, and all liars, shall have their part in the lake which burneth with fire and brimstone: which is the second death.*
> **Revelation 21:8 KJV**

The return of Jesus will be a glorious time for the church and all believers. It will be the final confirmation for all believers that their faith was fully justified. In the next chapter, we are going to look at some post end time prophecies, meaning prophecies of things that will take place following the return of Christ and the rapture of the church.

Chapter Eight
The Greatest Prophecy of All, The Return of Jesus Christ

Worksheet Questions for Chapter 8

1. What is the name of the tree that Adam and Eve were forbidden to eat from?

2. God named two trees in the Garden of Eden, what is the name of the other tree?

3. Following Adam and Eve's disobedience in the Garden of Eden, what human trait did all mankind inherit?

4. Why is Jesus qualified to save us from our sins and to cleanse us from our sin nature?

5. What are the three types of death?

6. What are the three components of a human being?

7. What does I Corinthians 15:44 tell us about bodies?

8. Where will the spirit go, for those who do not receive a glorified body?

Chapter Nine
Post End Time Prophecies

Thus far, we have looked at a lot of prophecies. Many of those prophecies have had to do with the time leading up to the rapture of the church or with the time during the great tribulation. But, the church as a whole doesn't focus much on the time following the rapture and the time following the tribulation, other than to sing and celebrate our spending eternity in heaven. But as we read in the Word, it seems God is telling us that He has some different plans for us.

What is Man's Purpose in Life?

God's plans for us, ultimately depends upon the choices we make while we are alive here on earth. Back in chapter eight, we talked a lot about the choices that Adam and Eve made back in the Garden of Eden. We talked about how those choices not only impacted their lives, but those choices also impacted the lives of all mankind.

While the choices we make certainly won't impact all mankind, they certainly will impact the future of the individual making them and those choices have a great potential of impacting the lives of other individuals around us as well. Through the centuries, philosophers, psychologists and others have written volumes on the meaning and purpose of life, hoping to help people make the right choices. The problem with most all of their writings is that their focus is on man's point of view. The purpose and meaning of man's existence on earth is not about what man wants, but it's about what God wants. We seem to always ask the right questions, what is my purpose in life, or what is the meaning of life. But, it seems we always get lost and frame the answer from

The Three Woes
A Guide To Understanding Revelation and End Time Prophecies

man's point of view and not from God's point of view. There's that sin nature getting in man's way again, always making everything about us and not about God.

The meaning and purpose of life is very simple when we get ourselves out of the way and answer the question from God's point of view. The answer goes right back to Adam and Eve. They were placed in the Garden of Eden so that God could determine if they would serve Him or if they would serve themselves by disobeying Him. The same is true for us today. God has placed us here to determine if we will chose to serve Him or if we will chose to serve ourselves.

Now, don't misunderstand, God will have other purposes for those who decide to serve Him. He will lead one into this profession and another into that vocation. But we're talking about the most basic root purpose of why man is on earth, and that purpose is for God to determine if each individual will chose to serve HIM or chose to serve themselves. God created man for fellowship with Himself. God desired to have a being who would voluntarily choose to love Him and to serve Him. That purpose hasn't changed since Adam and Eve. What has changed since Adam's fall is that man must now repent of his sins and seek forgiveness through Jesus Christ and His atoning blood to once again be in fellowship with God. The following flow chart is a simple logic diagram similar to what a computer programmer would use to begin programming a computer software program. Let's look at it and see what we can learn.

It seems that we can safely assume that we are living in the very last days before the rapture of the church. That places all mankind in the rectangular block at the top and center of the flow chart.

Chapter Nine
Post End Time Prophecies

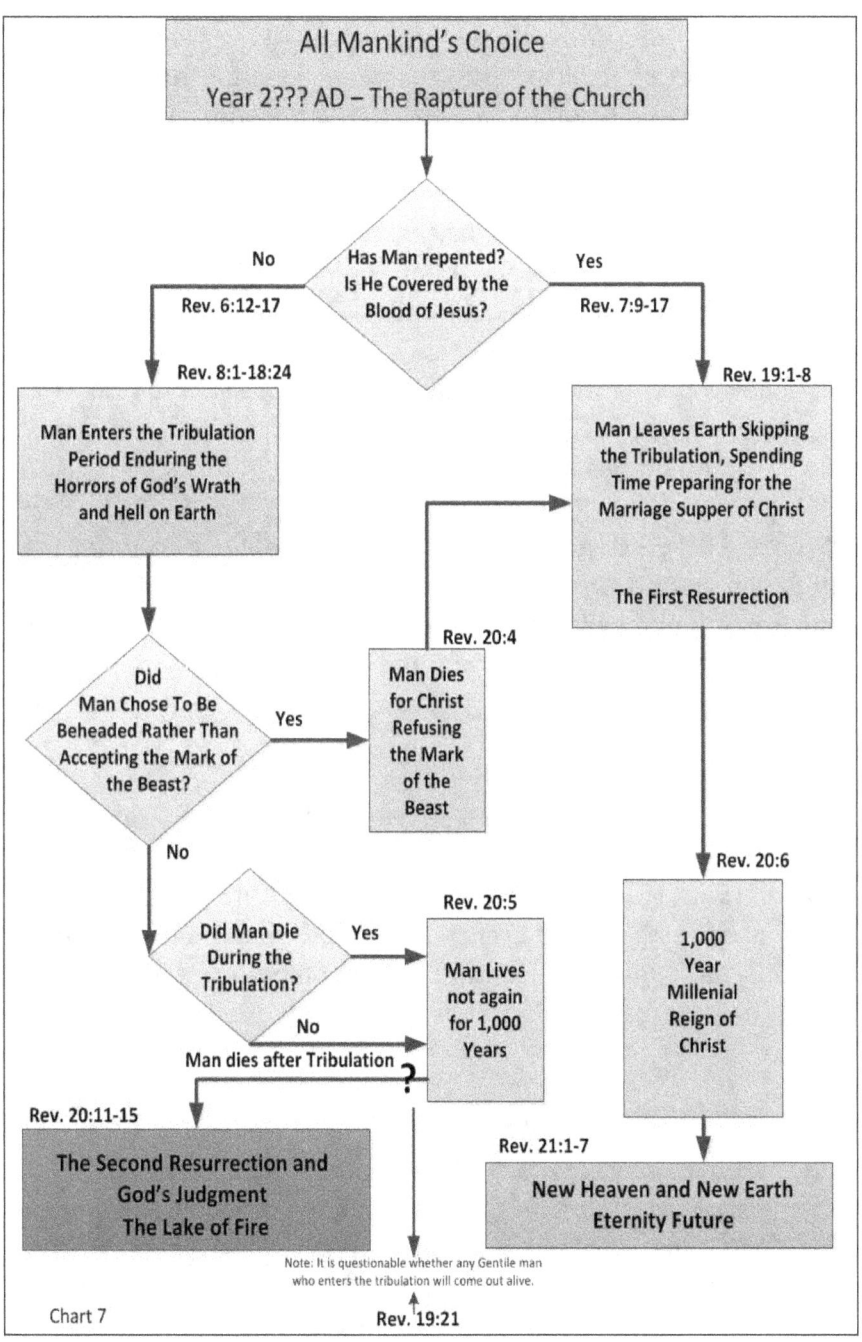

The Three Woes
A Guide To Understanding Revelation and End Time Prophecies

The only way out of that block is through what is called a decision block. The decision block asks a simple question and has two paths out, depending on the answer to the question. This decision block is asking about our relationship with God.

If any individual has not repented of their sins and confessed their sins, asking Jesus to save them, then they are going to follow the left hand branch in the diamond shaped decision block in the flow chart above. If they have given their life to Jesus then they will follow the right hand branch in the decision block. It is imperative for the wellbeing of man's eternal soul that he follows the right hand branch in the flow chart.

All those who chose the left hand branch are going to enter the tribulation period and experience the wrath and judgments of almighty God and eventually will spend eternity in the lake of fire. Once this path has been chosen, the only way to save one's life and soul is to be beheaded instead of taking the mark of the beast.

The Saints of God, Future Judges

What we want to focus on next, is what the future holds for those who chose the right hand branch in the flow chart above. Once an individual has chosen to take that right hand branch, they are now a part of that vast multitude we see described in Revelation Chapter 7.

> *After this I beheld, and, lo, a great multitude, which no man could number, of all nations, and kindreds, and people, and tongues, stood before the throne, and before the Lamb, clothed with white robes, and palms in their hands; 10 And cried with a loud voice, saying, Salvation to our God which sitteth upon the throne, and unto the Lamb.*

Chapter Nine
Post End Time Prophecies

11 And all the angels stood round about the throne, and about the elders and the four beasts, and fell before the throne on their faces, and worshipped God, 12 Saying, Amen: Blessing, and glory, and wisdom, and thanksgiving, and honour, and power, and might, be unto our God for ever and ever. Amen. 13 And one of the elders answered, saying unto me, What are these which are arrayed in white robes? and whence came they? 14 And I said unto him, Sir, thou knowest. And he said to me, These are they which came out of great tribulation, and have washed their robes, and made them white in the blood of the Lamb. 15 Therefore are they before the throne of God, and serve him day and night in his temple: and he that sitteth on the throne shall dwell among them. 16 They shall hunger no more, neither thirst any more; neither shall the sun light on them, nor any heat. 17 For the Lamb which is in the midst of the throne shall feed them, and shall lead them unto living fountains of waters: and God shall wipe away all tears from their eyes.

Revelation 7:9-17 KJV

The people we see described in these verses of Revelation are the raptured church, along with all the saints of God who died before the birth of Jesus. After this view of these saints in Heaven before God's throne, we don't see them again until Revelation Chapter 19 where they are about to attend the marriage supper of the Lamb. We know from our prior studies that these saints have now been in Heaven for more than seven years. Other than worshiping, God has not shared with us what they have been doing for these seven years. So let's look at what we do know.

The saints, the bride of Christ, will have a role to play in Christ's Millennial reign. Actually their role will be to help Christ usher in

His Millennial reign. In 1 Corinthians 6:2 & 3, we are told that the saints will judge the world and angels. We see further proof of this in the Book of Jude where we are told that the saints will not only judge, but will also execute judgment. That doesn't just mean pronounce judgment but it means to literally execute that judgment.

> *Do ye not know that the saints shall judge the world? and if the world shall be judged by you, are ye unworthy to judge the smallest matters? 3 Know ye not that we shall judge angels? how much more things that pertain to this life?*
> **1 Corinthians 6:2-3 KJV**

> *And Enoch also, the seventh from Adam, prophesied of these, saying, Behold, the Lord cometh with ten thousands of his saints, 15 To execute judgment upon all, and to convince all that are ungodly among them of all their ungodly deeds which they have ungodly committed, and of all their hard speeches which ungodly sinners have spoken against him.*
> **Jude 14-15 KJV**

As you read the verses in Jude, some might argue that the saints will not execute the convicted, that it will be Christ who will do the executing of judgment. So let's dig a little deeper and see what else the scriptures have to say about this matter. As we look at Psalms Chapter 149, we see further proof that it isn't just Christ who will execute the sentence, but it will also be the saints who will be carrying out the execution of justice. For those individuals in the world who only want to talk about the love of God, this Chapter in Psalms must seem incomprehensibly harsh and unloving.

Chapter Nine
Post End Time Prophecies

> *Let the saints be joyful in glory: let them sing aloud upon their beds. 6 Let the high praises of God be in their mouth, and a twoedged sword in their hand; 7 To execute vengeance upon the heathen, and punishments upon the people; 8 To bind their kings with chains, and their nobles with fetters of iron; 9 To execute upon them the judgment written: this honour have all his saints. Praise ye the Lord.*
> **Psalms 149:5-9 KJV**

Here in Psalms, God not only tells us that the saints will carry out justice, but God actually calls that justice vengeance. God clearly shows us that He is no respecter of persons. We see the vengeance of God directed not just at the common man, but also at kings and nobles. Nothing will gain a person a pass or pardon once judgment has been pronounced. The only time a pardon can be obtained is prior to the time when judgment is pronounced. Pardons only come through the blood of Jesus.

There is a question mark at the bottom of the flow chart with an arrow pointing to a note. The note is a question as to whether any Gentile who enters the tribulation time at its beginning will actually be able to live through it. The reason for that question mark and that line of thinking is the judgments that will be carried out by the saints. Due to the judgments pronounced, it is possible that the only individuals who will be allowed to come out of the tribulation period alive will be those who were born during the tribulation period and those converts of the house of Israel.

There is a passage of scripture in Daniel 12:10-12 that has puzzled theologians for years. Daniel references the 1,290 days that correlate to the 1,260 days of Revelation 13:5 and to Revelation 12:6. Daniel then says, blessed is anyone who comes to 1,335 days. For years now, Bible scholars have questioned the significance of these 45 days that Daniel speaks of.

> *Many shall be purified, and made white, and tried; but the wicked shall do wickedly: and none of the wicked shall understand; but the wise shall understand. 11 And from the time that the daily sacrifice shall be taken away, and the abomination that maketh desolate set up, there shall be a thousand two hundred and ninety days. 12 Blessed is he that waiteth, and cometh to the thousand three hundred and five and thirty days.*
> **Daniel 12:10-12 KJV**

While we can't say for sure, it seems as though it might be a reference to the transition time between the time Christ returns with His saints at the Battle of Armageddon and when the last of the Psalm Chapter 149 judgments are carried out. Many of us have had a concept that when Christ returns at the Battle of Armageddon, He would simply speak a Word and all His enemies would fall dead. But Psalms declares that Christ will use His saints to achieve His justice. Do these forty five days indicate the full duration of the Battle of Armageddon? Does it also indicate that the Jews who fled to the wilderness from the dragon in Revelation Chapter 12 will not be safe and secure until the completion of the 1,335 days? We can't know for sure, but it seems plausible.

> *And I saw heaven opened, and behold a white horse; and he that sat upon him was called Faithful and True, and in righteousness he doth judge and make war.* 12 His eyes were as a flame of fire, and on his head were many crowns; and he had a name written, that no man knew, but he himself. 13 *And he was clothed with a vesture dipped in blood: and his name is called The Word of God.* 14 And the armies which were in heaven followed him

Chapter Nine
Post End Time Prophecies

upon white horses, clothed in fine linen, white and clean. 15 And out of his mouth goeth a sharp sword, that with it he should smite the nations: and he shall rule them with a rod of iron: and he treadeth the winepress of the fierceness and wrath of Almighty God. 16 And he hath on his vesture and on his thigh a name written, KING OF KINGS, AND LORD OF LORDS. 17 And I saw an angel standing in the sun; and he cried with a loud voice, saying to all the fowls that fly in the midst of heaven, Come and gather yourselves together unto the supper of the great God; 18 That ye may eat the flesh of kings, and the flesh of captains, and the flesh of mighty men, and the flesh of horses, and of them that sit on them, and the flesh of all men, both free and bond, both small and great.
Revelation 19:11-18 KJV

The Conclusion of the Battle of Armageddon

At the conclusion of the Battle of Armageddon the false prophet, the beast, who is also called the Antichrist, and all who worshiped the image of the beast were cast alive into the lake of fire for all of eternity. The dragon who is the devil, Satan, is bound a thousand years and cast into the bottomless pit. At the end of the thousand years, he will be released to once again to deceive the nations for a period of time. As we look at the story of Satan's release from the bottomless pit, we see him engaging Gog and Magog to do battle with the saints of God. This Battle of Gog and Magog seems like it is probably what most people today call Ezekiel's war. We discussed this in depth back in chapter four.

And the beast was taken, and with him the false prophet that wrought miracles before him, with which he deceived them that had received the mark of the beast, and them

that worshipped his image. These both were cast alive into a lake of fire burning with brimstone.
Revelation 19:20 KJV

And he laid hold on the dragon, that old serpent, which is the Devil, and Satan, and bound him a thousand years, 3 And cast him into the bottomless pit, and shut him up, and set a seal upon him, that he should deceive the nations no more, till the thousand years should be fulfilled: and after that he must be loosed a little season.
Revelation 20:2-3 KJV

And when the thousand years are expired, Satan shall be loosed out of his prison, 8 And shall go out to deceive the nations which are in the four quarters of the earth, Gog and Magog, to gather them together to battle: the number of whom is as the sand of the sea.
Revelation 20:7-8 KJV

And the devil that deceived them was cast into the lake of fire and brimstone, where the beast and the false prophet are, and shall be tormented day and night for ever and ever.
Revelation 20:10 KJV

This war involving Gog and Magog is a very brief war at the end of the thousand year Millennial reign. The scripture only tells us that Satan and his followers encompass the saints and then God sends fire down from heaven and devours them. Satan is then cast into the lake of fire for ever and ever, where the antichrist and the false prophet have been for the past one thousand years.

Chapter Nine
Post End Time Prophecies

Post Millennial Reign

After the transition time following the return of Christ, all the saints will continue their function as judges and rulers with Christ during His Millennial reign. At the end of the Millennial reign, following Satan's brief release, we see God's new heaven and new earth. At this time, John also sees the New Jerusalem coming down from God out of heaven. John spends nearly a whole chapter in the Book of Revelation describing the New Jerusalem. This New Jerusalem is what most people are describing when they talk about what heaven will be like. What most of us hear about most is probably the streets of gold. It's interesting; the scripture only tells us about one street, singular. While there may be more streets, which is somewhat doubtful, we are not told that.

> *And the twelve gates were twelve pearls; every several gate was of one pearl: and the street of the city was pure gold, as it were transparent glass.*
> **Revelation 21:21 KJV**

> *And the city lieth foursquare, and the length is as large as the breadth: and he measured the city with the reed, twelve thousand furlongs. The length and the breadth and the height of it are equal.*
> **Revelation 21:16 KJV**

John provides a really detailed description of the city New Jerusalem. We are told that the city is actually a perfect cube that measures a little more than 1,377 miles on each side and in height. That is just a few miles less than the 1,386 miles that Detroit, Michigan is from Miami, Florida. The New Jerusalem has a wall around it that is over two hundred feet tall. There is far more that we could say to describe the city's physical characteristics but what we should probably focus on is the city's spiritual characteristics.

As we look at the scripture, we see that God is very clear about who will be in this city and who will not. The New Jerusalem is for the bride of Christ, those who have their names written in the Book of Life. It is not for those who have chosen to disobey God's commands. We can see in the scriptures below where God once again innumerate's a list of behaviors that will keep one from fellowship with God.

> *But the fearful, and unbelieving, and the abominable, and murderers, and whoremongers, and sorcerers, and idolaters, and all liars, shall have their part in the lake which burneth with fire and brimstone: which is the second death.*
> **Revelation 21:8 KJV**

> *And there shall in no wise enter into it any thing that defileth, neither whatsoever worketh abomination, or maketh a lie: but they which are written in the Lamb's book of life.*
> **Revelation 21:27 KJV**

> *For without are dogs, and sorcerers, and whoremongers, and murderers, and idolaters, and whosoever loveth and maketh a lie.*
> **Revelation 22:15 KJV**

> *And he shewed me a pure river of water of life, clear as crystal, proceeding out of the throne of God and of the Lamb. 2 In the midst of the street of it, and on either side of the river, was there the tree of life, which bare twelve*

Chapter Nine
Post End Time Prophecies

> *manner of fruits, and yielded her fruit every month: and the leaves of the tree were for the healing of the nations.*
> **Revelation 22:1-2 KJV**

That's really what it is all about, Fellowship with God. The New Jerusalem is God's replacement for the Garden of Eden. The tree of life is there, the water of life is there, God is there and man is there. This time though, only individuals who have had their sins washed away and covered by the blood of the Lamb, Jesus Christ, will be there.

> *And I heard a great voice out of heaven saying, Behold, the tabernacle of God is with men, and he will dwell with them, and they shall be his people, and God himself shall be with them, and be their God.*
> **Revelation 21:3 KJV**

So at this point in time, God has brought man full circle. God created man and placed man on the earth with dominion over the earth. But as we discussed earlier, when man sinned, Satan obtained temporary dominion over the earth. So what about that temporary dominion? In the next chapter, we are going to discuss what the seven sealed Book of Revelation Chapter 5 is all about.

Worksheet Questions for Chapter 9

1. According to God, what is man's purpose in life?

2. If an individual misses the rapture of the church and enters the tribulation period, what is their only means of escaping the lake of life?

3. What will the saints be doing during the 1,000 year Millennial Reign of Christ?

4. What do you think the extra 45 days of Daniel 12:10-12 are about?

5. What will happen at the conclusion of the Battle of Armageddon?

6. What happens at the end of the 1,000 year Millennial Reign of Christ?

Chapter Nine
Post End Time Prophecies

7. What is the outcome of the war that occurs at the end of the Millennial Reign?

8. What is it that most people call heaven?

9. What geometric shape is the city new Jerusalem?

10. What are the dimensions of each side of this city?

11. Who will be the residents of this city?

The Three Woes
A Guide To Understanding Revelation and End Time Prophecies

Chapter Ten
What Is the Seven Sealed Book of Revelation Chapter 5

We just saw, in the previous chapter, where God has created a new heaven and a new earth as well as the New Jerusalem. We also saw where God cast the antichrist and the false prophet into the lake of fire. And finally, we see God casting the devil into the lake of fire. So how did God deal with Satan's temporary dominion over the earth? Well, that's where the seven sealed book comes in.

Since, we are not explicitly told exactly what the book is, let's see if we can apply some logic to best answer that question. To do that, we will first look at some theories to see if they can be ruled out. One theory is that the seven sealed book contains the prophecies of the judgments of the tribulation period. This theory doesn't seem to make any sense, for the simple fact that the Book of Revelation is doing exactly that. Why would this book be duplicating the information that John is already providing us with in the Book of Revelation?

Another theory is that this is the Book of Life with the names of the saints written therein. This theory doesn't work because, as we look at the scriptures, we can see where God is continually in a process of adding and removing names from the Book of Life. When someone turns to God and has their sins covered by the blood of Jesus, their name is added to the Book of Life. When someone returns to a life of sin continuing to disobey God, then their name is removed from the Book of Life. God isn't sealing and unsealing the book in order to do this. Further, John wouldn't call it a seven sealed book; he would call it the Book of Life like he does on seven other times in the Book of Revelation. John refers to the Book of Life both before our introduction to the seven sealed book and also after its introduction. As explicit as John is in his writing, wouldn't he just say the Book of Life had seven seals? Certainly he would.

> *And I intreat thee also, true yokefellow, help those women which laboured with me in the gospel, with Clement also, and with other my fellowlabourers, whose names are in the book of life.*
> **Philippians 4:3 KJV**

> *He that overcometh, the same shall be clothed in white raiment; and I will not blot out his name out of the book of life, but I will confess his name before my Father, and before his angels.*
> **Revelation 3:5 KJV**

Yet another theory claims that the seven sealed book is the Word of Salvation and contains the final purposes of God to undo the curse of sin. If it is the Word of Salvation and it hasn't been opened yet, then how have men and women been getting saved through all the years since Jesus died on the cross? As to undoing the curse of sin, the verse below from Romans says that our old man is crucified with Christ and sin destroyed. So the curse of sin has already been dealt with through Christ's death on the cross. Nothing further needs to be done, Christ has provided our atonement and all we need to do is accept it.

> *Knowing this, that our old man is crucified with him, that the body of sin might be destroyed, that henceforth we should not serve sin.*
> **Romans 6:6 KJV**

Chapter Ten
What Is the Seven Sealed Book of Revelation Chapter 5

The Law of the Kinsman Redeemer

We probably haven't exhausted all the theories that people have put forth, but let's examine what seems to be the most logical and plausible explanation that is based on scripture, Jewish custom and Roman history. The seven sealed book is most likely the title deed to the earth and to all the property associated with the earth. Let's examine the Roman history, the Jewish customs and the scriptures in this respective order.

First, Roman history tells us that when a person wanted to leave a will, or a testament as they called it, they did so in the following manner. The testament was made in the presence of seven witnesses and each witness set their seal to the document or scroll to validate the will. If the document was not sealed with seven seals then the Roman court would invalidate the document. That is not too much different than how we do it today in our society, where we use two witnesses as proof that a last will and testament is valid.

Second, Jewish custom tells us that when a person lost his land due to a debt, the obligations required to reclaim the land were written on two scrolls. One scroll was unsealed so that it could be read and reviewed. It was stored in a public place within the Tabernacle. The other scroll was sealed with seven seals and held by the new owner of the land or in some other secure location for safe keeping by the new owner. The land or property described in the scroll could only be reclaimed by a qualified person. A kinsman redeemer who was willing to pay the price of redemption required to break the seven seals and satisfy the judgment lien identified within the scroll.

Third, let's look at some scriptures to see what God has told us in His word. Can we find scriptural support to go along with the

Roman history and the Jewish customs? To be thorough, let's look at both the Old Testament and the New Testament.

If we look at Leviticus 25:23, we see where God has told His chosen people that the land is not to be sold. Not only does God say that the land is not to be sold, He goes on to say that the land belongs to Him. When Adam sinned, man lost his right of dominion over the earth and Satan assumed that dominion. We also see where God instituted the concept of the kinsman redeemer in Verse 25.

> *The land shall not be sold for ever: for the land is mine; for ye are strangers and sojourners with me.*
> **Leviticus 25:23 KJV**

> *If thy brother be waxen poor, and hath sold away some of his possession, and if any of his kin come to redeem it, then shall he redeem that which his brother sold.*
> **Leviticus 25:25 KJV**

When we go to purchase a piece of property today, some properties are considered to be unimproved while others are improved. An unimproved property would be a piece of vacant land, while an improved property is considered to be one that has a structure of some type on it. Man was God's improvement to planet earth. If we look at Colossians Chapter 1 and Hebrews Chapter 9, we see where the death of God's Son paid the redemptive price for mankind's transgressions. Not only did God need to reclaim the land that was lost through sin, but God also needed to pay the price for mankind's sin through the shedding of blood.

Chapter Ten
What Is the Seven Sealed Book of Revelation Chapter 5

In whom we have redemption through his blood, even the forgiveness of sins:
Colossians 1:14 KJV

And for this cause he is the mediator of the new testament, that by means of death, for the redemption of the transgressions that were under the first testament, they which are called might receive the promise of eternal inheritance. 16 For where a testament is, there must also of necessity be the death of the testator. 17 For a testament is of force after men are dead: otherwise it is of no strength at all while the testator liveth.
Hebrews 9:15-17 KJV

As we have said, the possession that God really wants back is man. Man is God's prized possession. But, just like today, if a mortgage lender forecloses on someone's house, their home, the only way that the original owner can regain ownership of the home, is to satisfy the mortgage lien that the lender has against the land that the home sets on. That is why the seven sealed book appears to be the mortgage instrument that Christ must satisfy to reclaim His rightful ownership of both the earth and of man.

Christ, Our Kinsman Redeemer

God desired man and desired to have fellowship with man, and God was willing to pay the price to reclaim man and to redeem man. According to the law of the kinsman redeemer, the new owner of the land could not keep the land if the original owner had the means to pay the price to redeem the land. In Peter, we are told that Christ died; shedding His sinless blood to redeem us from the debt of sin we are all bound to. We only need to avail ourselves of His redemption.

> Forasmuch as ye know that ye were not redeemed with corruptible things, as silver and gold, from your vain conversation received by tradition from your fathers; 19 But with the precious blood of Christ, as of a lamb without blemish and without spot:
> **1 Peter 1:18-19 KJV**

> *For there is one God, and one mediator between God and men, the man Christ Jesus; 6 Who gave himself a ransom for all, to be testified in due time.*
> **1 Timothy 2:5-6 KJV**

The seven sealed book, here in Revelation, is the redemption paper for reclaiming the earth that was lost to Satan by Adam when he committed sin in the Garden of Eden. God gave Adam authority over the earth and over all creatures on the earth but when Adam sinned; he relinquished that authority to Satan as shown in Luke 4:5-6 when Jesus was tempted of the Devil.

> *And the devil, taking him up into an high mountain, shewed unto him all the kingdoms of the world in a moment of time. 6 And the devil said unto him, All this power will I give thee, and the glory of them: for that is delivered unto me; and to whomsoever I will I give it.*
> **Luke 4:5-6 KJV**

So why didn't God just send an angelic being like Michael or Gabriel to redeem man? The answer to that is very simple. The redeemer had to be a man; the redeemer had to be a part of the human race. The law of the kinsman redeemer specified that the redeemer had to be a qualified relative. This is why John wept

Chapter Ten
What Is the Seven Sealed Book of Revelation Chapter 5

when initially no man was found to open the book. He knew an angel wouldn't do, the redeemer had to be a man. As we said earlier, the hope of the Christian church and even of the whole world is dependent on a kinsman redeemer being able to open this seven sealed book in order to redeem mankind.

> *And one of the elders saith unto me, Weep not: behold, the Lion of the tribe of Juda, the Root of David, hath prevailed to open the book, and to loose the seven seals thereof. 6 And I beheld, and, lo, in the midst of the throne and of the four beasts, and in the midst of the elders, stood a Lamb as it had been slain, having seven horns and seven eyes, which are the seven Spirits of God sent forth into all the earth.*
> **Revelation 5:5-6 KJV**

When Christ was born of the Virgin Mary, He met the condition of being a kinsman redeemer because He became a part of the human race. When Christ died a sinless death on the cross, He earned the right to redeem the earth back from Satan. Jesus earned not only the right to redeem the earth but to also redeem God's lost possession, mankind. The shedding of His innocent and worthy blood legally discharged the lien on the souls of all men. Christ earned the right to redeem the earth and mankind over two thousand years ago, but He has not yet claimed that right. As we have said and proved throughout this book, the seals are in the process of being opened, but that opening process is not yet complete. When we see the words "It is done" in Revelation 16:17, the angel is telling us that the last seal has been opened and that the redemption, reclaiming and cleansing of the earth is complete.

The seven sealed book is the title deed to the earth and to man, God's improvement to the earth. In Old Testament time, when a kinsman was ready to redeem a property, they would take ten elders as witnesses to the payment to satisfy the lien. What we see here in Revelation Chapter 5, after Christ takes the seven sealed book out of the hand of God and begins to open the seals, is the four beasts and the four and twenty elders falling down before God's throne and before the Lamb. There, they proclaim that the Lamb, who will hence forth be called the Lion of the tribe of Judah, is worthy to take the book and to open the seals thereof. The four beasts and the four and twenty elders are Christ's witnesses to His payment to reclaim that which had been lost. Jesus, the Lamb, the Lion of the tribe of Judah, has redeemed us to God by His blood.

> *And when he had taken the book, the four beasts and four and twenty elders fell down before the Lamb, having every one of them harps, and golden vials full of odours, which are the prayers of saints. 9 And they sung a new song, saying, Thou art worthy to take the book, and to open the seals thereof: for thou wast slain, and hast redeemed us to God by thy blood out of every kindred, and tongue, and people, and nation;*
> **Revelation 5:8-9 KJV**

As we have said, the last seal has not yet been opened. So if that last seal has not been opened yet, then how does man currently avail himself of God's redemption? We are told in Ephesians 1:13-14 that the Holy Spirit is the down payment of our purchase by Christ until the last seal has been opened and the title deed claimed.

> *In whom ye also trusted, after that ye heard the word of truth, the gospel of your salvation: in whom also after that ye believed, ye were sealed with that holy Spirit of promise, 14 Which is the earnest of our inheritance until the*

Chapter Ten
What Is the Seven Sealed Book of Revelation Chapter 5

redemption of the purchased possession, unto the praise of his glory.
Ephesians 1:13-14 KJV

When Adam sinned, he lost the title deed of earth to Satan. When Christ died on the cross He earned the right to take back that title deed from Satan and it is now in God's hands waiting for it to be opened by Jesus Christ, the Lion of the tribe of Judah. In the Gospels of Matthew, Mark, Luke and John, we see four titles given to Jesus. He is the Son of David, the Son of Abraham, the Son of Man and the Son of God. As the Son of David, He has the right to claim title to the Throne of David. As the Son of Abraham, He has the right to claim title to the Land of Israel, as defined in Genesis. As the Son of Man, He has the right to claim title to the Earth. As the Son of God, He is the Heir of All Things.

Soon that last seal will be opened and Jesus Christ, the Lion from the Tribe of Judah is going to step forth claiming His titles, claiming His possessions and initiating His one thousand year reign from the city of Jerusalem. In the next chapter, we are going to conclude this book by looking at how we can best prepare ourselves to be ready for that glorious day.

The Three Woes
A Guide To Understanding Revelation and End Time Prophecies

Worksheet Questions for Chapter 10

1. What is God's most prized possession?

2. What is the law of the kinsman redeemer?

3. Why didn't God send an angel to reclaim the earth and to redeem mankind?

4. What qualified Christ to be our kinsman redeemer?

5. Christ has earned the right to reclaim the earth and to redeem mankind, but has He claimed that right?

6. What is the purpose of the four beasts and the four and twenty elders in Revelation Chapter 5?

Chapter Ten
What Is the Seven Sealed Book of Revelation Chapter 5

7. If that last seal has not been opened yet, then how does man currently avail himself of God's redemption?

8. What are the four titles given to Jesus in the Gospels?

The Three Woes
A Guide To Understanding Revelation and End Time Prophecies

Chapter Eleven
Conclusion

Thus far, we have looked at a lot of prophecies and reviewed a lot of scriptures. And while you may not agree with every view point of this book, the one thing that most of us do agree on is that spiritually speaking, time is short. It seems everywhere you look people are noticing signs and there is a general feeling that something is about to happen. The question is, What do we do about it? That's a very good question, because if we don't ask that question it is very likely that we will simply continue on as we are and do nothing about it.

This Is Our Season

Not too long ago, a southern gospel group called "Voice of Hope Trio" released a song titled "This Is Our Season." The song's title is taken from Ecclesiastes 3:1 through 8 where King Solomon lists various activities that most of us will experience at some point during our life. The title of that song seems exceptionally appropriate for all of us today. **This Is Our Season!** It is our time to seek God's face. It is our time to call on God. No matter where we might think we stand with God, we can all benefit by drawing closer to God.

> *To every thing there is a season, and a time to every purpose under the heaven: 2 A time to be born, and a time to die; a time to plant, and a time to pluck up that which is planted; 3 A time to kill, and a time to heal; a time to break down, and a time to build up; 4 A time to weep, and a time to laugh; a time to mourn, and a time to dance; 5 A time to cast away stones, and a time to gather stones together; a time to embrace, and a time to refrain from embracing; 6*

The Three Woes
A Guide To Understanding Revelation and End Time Prophecies

> *A time to get, and a time to lose; a time to keep, and a time to cast away; 7 A time to rend, and a time to sew; a time to keep silence, and a time to speak; 8 A time to love, and a time to hate; a time of war, and a time of peace.*
> **Ecclesiastes 3:1-8 KJV**

The hardest thing for any of us to see is our own faults. Take an alcoholic for example. The most difficult part of an alcoholic's recovery is getting him to admit that he is an alcoholic. It seems that we as Christians aren't too much different from the alcoholic. Remember back in chapter 6, where we reviewed the letters to the churches in Revelation Chapters 2 & 3, and concluded that they were not only real churches in John's day, but that they were also symbolic of the church age. The last church, the end time church, the Laodicean church, was the church that received Christ's harshest and sternest warning.

> *And unto the angel of the church of the Laodiceans write; These things saith the Amen, the faithful and true witness, the beginning of the creation of God; 15 I know thy works, that thou art neither cold nor hot: I would thou wert cold or hot. 16 So then because thou art lukewarm, and neither cold nor hot, I will spue thee out of my mouth. 17 Because thou sayest, I am rich, and increased with goods, and have need of nothing; and knowest not that thou art wretched, and miserable, and poor, and blind, and naked: 18 I counsel thee to buy of me gold tried in the fire, that thou mayest be rich; and white raiment, that thou mayest be clothed, and that the shame of thy nakedness do not appear; and anoint thine eyes with eyesalve, that thou mayest see. 19 As many as I love, I rebuke and chasten: be zealous therefore, and repent.*
> **Revelation 3:14-19 KJV**

Chapter Eleven
Conclusion

The Laodicean church is much like the alcoholic that doesn't know that he is a wretched drunkard. The Laodicean church member says that he has need of nothing but can't see that he is wretched, and miserable, and poor, and blind, and naked. Just like the alcoholic, the hardest part in getting the Laodicean church member the help he needs, is to get him to admit his need. For many, going to church has become a social event instead of a spiritual experience. For many, going to church is a habitual routine not a holy rite. For many, living and acting differently, out of church than in church, is an accepted norm when it should be an unacceptable exception.

The point is, God wants a holy church, a holy people, without spot or wrinkle. A people exemplifying a life that Christ Himself would live if He were walking in our shoes today. The great news is, we can be that church if we choose to. We don't have to be a Laodicean church member. Remember, This Is Our Season! If we don't know Christ and His salvation, we can call on Him while He is yet here to be found. In Romans, we are told that if we will turn from our wicked ways and confess our sins to Jesus, and believe in our heart that God raised Jesus from the dead, then we shall be saved. All we need to do at that point is to confess our salvation with our mouth.

> *That he might present it to himself a glorious church, not having spot, or wrinkle, or any such thing; but that it should be holy and without blemish.*
> **Ephesians 5:27 KJV**

> *That if thou shalt confess with thy mouth the Lord Jesus, and shalt believe in thine heart that God hath raised him from the dead, thou shalt be saved. 10 For with the heart*

man believeth unto righteousness; and with the mouth confession is made unto salvation.
Romans 10:9-10 KJV

If you already know Jesus and His salvation but feel there is room for you to draw nearer to Him, then you're not alone. We all have room to draw closer to Jesus and to be more Christ like in our daily walk with Him. God is long suffering and merciful toward us all. He will work with us through our entire lives to shape us into what He wants us to be spiritually. The only thing required on our part is to be willing and obedient servants. Now is the time of salvation, now is the time to draw nearer to God, this is our season!

The Ten Commandments

So, let's pause a moment and take a better look at the condition of the Laodicean church. Let's do so through a very simple set of God's commands, they are called the Ten Commandments. The Ten Commandments are a set of biblical laws relating to morals and worship. The Ten Commandments appear twice in the Old Testament, once in the Book of Exodus Chapter 20 and once in the Book of Deuteronomy Chapter 5. The history of the Ten Commandments in American society dates back prior to the landing of the Mayflower at Plymouth Rock in 1620. So the commandments are not only a part of the Bible and Jewish society but also a major part of our American society from its very beginnings.

Examining the Spiritual Health of Our Society

The Ten Commandments are a good reference point to measure not only the spiritual health of the Laodicean church in our society, but also the spiritual health of our American society in

Chapter Eleven
Conclusion

general. If we look back at the early days following America's independence, we see evidence of the Ten Commandments and other Judeo-Christian symbols and scriptures mingled throughout America's most prominent landmarks. The Supreme Court, Washington's Monument, Jefferson's Memorial, the US Capital Building, the Library of Congress and even the National Archives all have numerous references to America's spiritual heritage displayed in either statues, paintings, engravings, inscriptions or plaques. But since the latter half of the twentieth century, there has been an ongoing assault to discredit America's ties to its spiritual heritage.

Some of these individuals who are rewriting history are the same ones who scream "separation of church and state" and want to abolish any reference to Christianity in our society. It's easy to see that our founding fathers did indeed establish a "separation of church and state" when they set in place the new republic. The problem is that the anti-faith, anti-god based segment of our society has worked diligently to twist the meaning and intent of the freedom loving, God fearing, patriotic founding fathers.

The founding fathers intentions were to keep the state out of the church not the church out of the state. Remember, for many of them, it was their ancestors that fled the old world seeking the freedom to worship as they chose without the interference of king or government. Did they all believe the same way, and all have the exact same theological beliefs? Absolutely not! That was the whole intent, that each individual could worship and express his or her own spiritual beliefs without the interference of any ruling body or individual. The new state was made up of individuals and many of those individuals had strong beliefs in God and carried those beliefs with them into office as they governed. Their clear intent was to create a society where the people could freely worship God and express their love of God,

The Three Woes
A Guide To Understanding Revelation and End Time Prophecies

where the state would not dictate the manner or form of that expression. The state's duty is to provide a free expression of faith, but what we have today is a state that is attempting to expunge any religious expression from all aspects of our society.

Let's look at a few examples of this. First of all, let's look at a simple subject like marriage. In today's society, marriage is seen as an institution of the state. A couple will go to a state agency, pay a fee and obtain a license from the state to marry. In most ancient societies, the institution of marriage became the secure environment required for the perpetuation of the species. By the 1500s, there appeared to be many marriages taking place without a witness or ceremony. The Roman Catholic Church at the Council of Trent was so disturbed by this that they decreed in 1563 that marriages should be celebrated in the presence of a priest and at least two witnesses. Until the 1500s, the Catholic Church accepted a couple's word that they had exchanged marriage vows, with no witnesses or corroborating evidence needed. Early in the United States, some protestant churches accepted marriage based on the statement of a man and a woman agreeing to live in a marital state, while others required a ceremony before a member of the clergy. By the nineteenth century marriage licenses were common in the United States and today a church can't perform a marriage without a state license and the clergy member frequently needs to be licensed by the state. The state is now in the process of redefining marriage so that it is no longer limited to a union between a man and a woman. What was once an agreement between a man and a woman and recognized by the church, has become the dominion of the state.

So what about education in America? In colonial America, it was common for children to be home schooled or for the schools to be run by churches. The Pilgrims and other settlers recognized the importance for children to be able to read, write and have basic

Chapter Eleven
Conclusion

math skills. As part of the daily curriculum, students were taught to pray and read the Bible. In the late 1600s, the "New England Primer" was introduced which taught spelling, reading and the alphabet using Bible verses. Bible verses were used to teach the student right from wrong and to develop good moral character. Yale, which was founded in 1701, adopted a Hebrew insignia, and the Hebrew language was compulsory at Harvard until 1787. After America's Revolution, Noah Webster introduced the "Blue Book Speller," it too used Bible verses to teach reading and spelling. In 1836 the "McGuffey Reader" came along and it too featured Bible verses to teach reading and good moral values. The schools in America continued to be run mostly by Christian Churches until the late 1800s. In the 1890s, the states started to take control of the existing schools as many churches turned their schools over to the state run educational system. At the beginning of the Twentieth Century, many classrooms started each day with the pledge of allegiance, a prayer and a scripture reading from the Bible. By the end of the Twentieth Century, prayer had been banned from the classroom and any public functions of the school, including sports and social activities. The Twentieth Century has also seen the teaching of the theory of evolution and the Biblical story of the Creation has been banned. So what we have in the Twentieth Century is a state that has made it illegal for a child not to attend school yet that student has been forbidden their right to worship or call upon their God while doing so. The same state government that was originally founded to provide freedom of religion has twisted the founding fathers' concept to mean freedom from religion.

Let's look at the Internal Revenue Service and the 501C tax code. But before we look at the tax code, it would be good to review how the IRS came to be. The first income tax was a temporary tax levied in 1862 by the Union to pay for the cost of the Civil War. In 1872, the lawmakers allowed the temporary Civil War tax to expire. In 1894 lawmakers once again implemented an income tax, but it was challenged and declared unconstitutional by the Supreme Court. In 1913 the Sixteenth Amendment to the Constitution was ratified allowing the government to collect taxes on income. The entity Americans know as the IRS came to be in 1913.

Prior to 1954, churches were automatically exempt from taxation, but in 1954 Senator Lyndon B. Johnson introduced a bill that became law. This bill made it illegal for a church to openly speak out against anything that the government declared "legal," even if it is immoral, such as abortion or homosexuality, etc. If a church willingly does so, that church jeopardizes its tax exempt status. What exists is a situation where the state can impose its will upon the church by passing unconstitutional laws that limit the freedom of church leaders to express their views on certain issues. If the view of the church and the state are in conflict, then the state has the power to financially penalize the church. The end effect is that free speech within the church is under attack and the churches voice against sin has been stifled.

Since colonial days, our country has had Blue Laws. A Blue Law is a law that prohibits commercial activity on Sunday. Many states and towns passed laws to forbid merchants and laborers from working on Sunday. These laws were not based on concerns that workers deserved a day of rest. Instead, they were meant to respect the Christian Sabbath and were directed at personal activities regarded as moral offenses, such as gambling or the consumption of alcohol. In the nineteenth century, the enactment of these laws proceeded west with the expansion of the United States. Prior to the twentieth century most all non-essential businesses were closed on Sunday. Only hospitals, inns for lodging and feeding guests and a few other necessary businesses were open for business.

Chapter Eleven
Conclusion

From 1859 to 1900 the Supreme Court heard eight cases concerning blue laws. Then, in 1961 the Supreme Court resolved the constitutionality of blue laws by ruling that the laws had been established since the 1700s for nonreligious reasons. The Court acknowledged that historically the laws had a religious motivation and were designed to promote the concepts of Christian theology. The Court then ruled that the law did not infringed on an individual's religious freedom but that it only caused financial loss. The Blue Laws survived the Supreme Court but they have all but died in the face of America's moral decline. The only Blue Laws that remain are the few related to Sunday liquor sales.

So despite the attempt to alter history, the evidence still points to the fact that America's founding fathers intentionally worked to establish a new type of republic; A republic based on Judeo-Christian principals and morals, A republic that believed in the biblical God of Israel, A republic that believed in God's Ten Commandments and God's moral laws, A republic that derived its power from God and a republic that must answer to God morally, A republic that established freedom of religion not freedom from religion.

Examining the Spiritual Health of the Church

So exactly what are these Ten Commandments that the atheists and the anti-god groups hate and fear so much? As the name implies, there are ten of them and they are commands. One might also think of them as laws, or rules or instructions. Much like how a parent might instruct a child. The Ten Commandments can easily be divided into two groups. The first four commandments deal with man's relationship to God and the last six deal with man's relationship to his fellow man. It seems that most of America today, including many of those associated with some church body tends to totally ignore the commandments of God.

The Three Woes
A Guide To Understanding Revelation and End Time Prophecies

The only commandments they follow are those commandments that have penalties attached to them according to America's civil law. One might argue that the only commandments the typical American follows are number 6, thou shalt not murder and number 8, thou shalt not steal. Then it might be questioned, are the commandments being kept or simply civil law? A list of the Ten Commandments is shown below in a shortened format.

THE TEN COMMANDMENTS IN A SHORTENED FORMAT	
1	You shall have no other gods before Me.
2	You shall not make idols.
3	You shall not take the name of the LORD your God in vain.
4	Remember the Sabbath day, to keep it holy.
5	Honor your father and your mother.
6	You shall not murder.
7	You shall not commit adultery.
8	You shall not steal.
9	You shall not bear false witness against your neighbor.
10	You shall not covet.

When you think of the Ten Commandments, what is the first one that comes to your mind? Is it "thou shalt not kill (murder)?" When you give your child a list of chores or duties to be performed, how do you prioritize the list? Do you put the least important chore or duty first? No, of course not. You put the most important one first, then followed by the one you consider to be next in importance. The order of importance to your child never enters your thinking. You would say, "make your bed and clean your room, when you are finished with that, cut the grass, then you can go play with your friends." If you returned to find the grass uncut and the bed unmade, you would probably be very upset and ready to administer some justice.

Chapter Eleven
Conclusion

We are all made in the image of God, so the way God deals with us is not much different than how we deal with our children. God gave us the commandments and listed them in the order of importance to Him. First and foremost, He commands us to have no other gods before Him; not our family, not our job, not some sports team, and not some television program or video game.

It is also interesting to note that God elaborated quite a bit when it came to certain commandments. Note in particular the fourth commandment concerning the Sabbath day. Both in Exodus and Deuteronomy, God tells us to "remember the Sabbath day to keep it holy," then He continues on for three verses being specific on how we should do that.

> *Remember the sabbath day, to keep it holy. 9 Six days shalt thou labour, and do all thy work: 10 But the seventh day is the sabbath of the Lord thy God: in it thou shalt not do any work, thou, nor thy son, nor thy daughter, thy manservant, nor thy maidservant, nor thy cattle, nor thy stranger that is within thy gates: 11 For in six days the Lord made heaven and earth, the sea, and all that in them is, and rested the seventh day: wherefore the Lord blessed the sabbath day, and hallowed it.*
> **Exodus 20:8-11 KJV**

How does our society honor the Sabbath day? How does the church honor and remember the Sabbath day? How do you honor and remember the Sabbath day? In Jeremiah 17:19-27 the prophet Jeremiah tells the people of Judah God's instructions on how to honor the Sabbath day.

> *Thus said the Lord unto me; Go and stand in the gate of the children of the people, whereby the kings of Judah come in, and by the which they go out, and in all the gates*

of Jerusalem; 20 And say unto them, Hear ye the word of the Lord, ye kings of Judah, and all Judah, and all the inhabitants of Jerusalem, that enter in by these gates: 21 Thus saith the Lord; Take heed to yourselves, and bear no burden on the sabbath day, nor bring it in by the gates of Jerusalem; 22 Neither carry forth a burden out of your houses on the sabbath day, neither do ye any work, but hallow ye the sabbath day, as I commanded your fathers. 23 But they obeyed not, neither inclined their ear, but made their neck stiff, that they might not hear, nor receive instruction. 24 And it shall come to pass, if ye diligently hearken unto me, saith the Lord, to bring in no burden through the gates of this city on the sabbath day, but hallow the sabbath day, to do no work therein; 25 Then shall there enter into the gates of this city kings and princes sitting upon the throne of David, riding in chariots and on horses, they, and their princes, the men of Judah, and the inhabitants of Jerusalem: and this city shall remain for ever. 26 And they shall come from the cities of Judah, and from the places about Jerusalem, and from the land of Benjamin, and from the plain, and from the mountains, and from the south, bringing burnt offerings, and sacrifices, and meat offerings, and incense, and bringing sacrifices of praise, unto the house of the Lord. 27 But if ye will not hearken unto me to hallow the sabbath day, and not to bear a burden, even entering in at the gates of Jerusalem on the sabbath day; then will I kindle a fire in the gates thereof, and it shall devour the palaces of Jerusalem, and it shall not be quenched.
Jeremiah 17:19-27 KJV

So what does the health of the Laodicean church look like? It looks like it is on life support. And what did Jesus say about it in Revelation 3:15 & 16? *I know thy works, that thou art neither cold*

Chapter Eleven
Conclusion

nor hot: I would thou wert cold or hot. So then because thou art lukewarm, and neither cold nor hot, I will spue thee out of my mouth. The good news is, **This Is Our Season!** We can still reach out to God and seek His face. Remember Christ is seeking a bride without spot or wrinkle and no unclean thing will enter into heaven.

> *For this ye know, that no whoremonger, nor unclean person, nor covetous man, who is an idolater, hath any inheritance in the kingdom of Christ and of God.*
> **Ephesians 5:5 KJV**

> *Know ye not that the unrighteous shall not inherit the kingdom of God? Be not deceived: neither fornicators, nor idolaters, nor adulterers, nor effeminate, nor abusers of themselves with mankind, 10 Nor thieves, nor covetous, nor drunkards, nor revilers, nor extortioners, shall inherit the kingdom of God.*
> **1 Corinthians 6:9-10 KJV**

The Biblical Path Back to God

What does the Bible have to say about backsliding and returning to God? In the Book of Jeremiah, we see the prophet Jeremiah warning Judah and the people of Israel of God's coming judgment against the nation. After the death of King Josiah, the last righteous king for the nation of Judah, we see King Nebuchadnezzar conquering Judah and the people of Israel were taken into Babylonian captivity.

So how did the people go about returning to God and seeking His mercies once again? If we look at the Book of Nehemiah the scriptures give us a picture of how the people humbled their hearts and sought God's forgiveness and mercies. In Nehemiah 9:1 & 2 we see where the children of Israel took their first step back toward God by fasting and confessing the sins and iniquities of their fathers.

> *Now in the twenty and fourth day of this month the children of Israel were assembled with fasting, and with sackclothes, and earth upon them. 2 And the seed of Israel separated themselves from all strangers, and stood and confessed their sins, and the iniquities of their fathers.*
> **Nehemiah 9:1-2 KJV**

The second step in Israel's journey back to God is found in Nehemiah 9:3 where we are told that the people read the Book of the Law one fourth part of the day. We are also told that the people spent another one fourth part of the day confessing their sins and worshiping the Lord their God.

> *And they stood up in their place, and read in the book of the law of the Lord their God one fourth part of the day; and another fourth part they confessed, and worshipped the Lord their God.*
> **Nehemiah 9:3 KJV**

The third step back to God involved action on the part of the people. In Nehemiah 9:38 and 10:28-32 the people made a covenant to keep the law as given by Moses and to live in a certain manner (See Nehemiah 9:13 & 14).

For many years America has enjoyed God's blessings of being God's chosen nation among the Gentiles. Our path back to God lies in our reading and studying God's Word and then confessing the sins of the nation and praising and worshiping God. America needs to get back to the basics, the ten laws given to Moses by

Chapter Eleven
Conclusion

God, The Ten Commandments. Our path back to God will require of us that we read God's Word, and reading it means to study it and hide it in our hearts, not just reading the words, while our mind is thinking about something else.

Second, we will need to spend time in prayer and seek God's face, giving Him praise and worshiping Him. We need to make Him first and foremost in our life.

Third, we should begin confessing the sins of the nation. We need to be specific and ask God to forgive us for placing other gods before Him. We need to confess the sin of setting up idols. We need to confess the sin of taking God's name in vain, and this doesn't mean just cursing, but it means claiming to be a Christian when we live like the devil. We need to confess our sin of failing to remember the Sabbath day. We need to confess our sin of murdering millions of our unborn youth.

This is God's scriptural example of how we as a nation, and church, can return to Him.

This Is Our Season! It is for us to do it. Time is short.

The Three Woes
A Guide To Understanding Revelation and End Time Prophecies

Worksheet Questions for Chapter 11

1. What was the purpose for the separation of church and state?

2. Can you see how America's school system has gone from being a spiritual based system run by the churches, to a secular based system run by the government?

3. What happened in 1954 that helped to stifle the churches voice against sin?

4. What is a Blue Law and what is its purpose?

5. Is America honoring God's Sabbath in a manner pleasing to Him?

6. How did the people of Israel go about seeking God following the destruction of Israel and their Babylonian captivity?

Work Sheet Answers

The Three Woes
A Guide To Understanding Revelation and End Time Prophecies

Worksheet Answers for Chapter 1

Answer 1:
Enos was Adam's Grandson.

Answer 2:
Adam was 265 years old when Enos celebrated his 30th birthday.

Answer 3:
Enos was 695 years old when his grandfather Adam died.

Answer 4:
We know that all the information within Genesis prior to Noah's flood had to have been passed down to us in this manner, by word of mouth. Did Adam share more stories with Enos about what life was like for himself and Eve in the Garden of Eden? Sadness for eating from the tree of knowledge of good and evil and eating from the tree of life. Did he share about how easy life was in the garden and how hard and difficult it was outside the garden? Did Adam share about how their relationship with God was so different than it was before?

Answer 5:
Enos was 851 years old when Noah celebrated his 30th birthday.

Answer 6:
Noah was 84 years old when Enos died.

Answer 7:
We saw where Enos had the opportunity of learning much from his grandfather Adam. Noah had even greater opportunities. Noah had five generations of great grandparents to learn from. A sixth great grandparent would have been Enoch, but Enoch was

taken by God just 69 years before Noah was born. We know Enoch walked with God, he was a man with a close relationship with God and also Methuselah's father. Methuselah was Noah's grandfather. What spiritual insights did Methuselah share with Noah? Did he tell Noah about seeing his father Enoch taken up to God like Elijah? Did he describe his father's relationship with God? Did tell stories about how God helped and blessed his father?

Answer 8:
Methusalah, the oldest living human died at the age of 969 years.

Answer 9:
In Genesis 7:11, we told that the great flood began when the fountains of the deep were broken up and the windows of heaven were opened. We are specifically told that this occurred in the second month and the seventeenth day of the month. This was not according to the Gregorian calendar, it didn't exist. It is not clear whether it is second month and the seventeenth day following Noah's birthday or the second month and the seventeenth day of the Jewish calendar, but most likely the latter.

Answer 10:
Joseph was born 2259 years after Adam was created.

Gen. 37:2	Joseph was 17 years old when he was sold into bondage.
Gen 41:29-30	Seven good years followed by seven years of famine.
Gen. 41:46	Joseph was 30 years old when he stood before pharaoh.
Gen. 45:6	Famine had been in the land for two years when Jacob came to Egypt.
Gen. 47:9	Jacob was 130 years old when he stood before pharaoh.

The Three Woes
A Guide To Understanding Revelation and End Time Prophecies

7	Seven good years
+2	Two years of famine

9	Total good and bad years before Jacob came to Egypt

130	The age Jacob was when he stood before pharaoh
-9	Total good and bad years before Jacob came to Egypt

121	Jacob's age when Joseph stood before pharaoh

2168	Jacob was born in this year after Adam's creation
+ 121	Jacob's age when Joseph stood before pharaoh

2289	
-30	Joseph's age when he stood before pharaoh

2259	The year Joseph was born following Adam's creation

Answer 11:
Joseph was 30 years when he stood before pharaoh and became second in command over all of Egypt.

Answer 12:
According to the Hebrew Bible and calendar, man has been on earth for 5,781 years.

Work Sheet Answers

Worksheet Answers for Chapter 2

Answer 1:
The seven divisions of the Book of Revelation are:

1. Chapter 1	The Addresses to the Churches
2. Chapter 2 & 3	The Introduction and Salutation
3. Chapter 4	The Beginning of John's Vision
4. Chapter 5 - 18	The Seven Seals
5. Chapter 19	The Marriage Supper of the Lamb
6. Chapter 20	The Millennial Reign of Christ
7. Chapter 21 & 22	The Post Millennium Reign

Answer 2:
The three Woes of Revelation 8:13 are the 5th, 6th and 7th Trumpet Angels that will sound their trumpet in Revelation Chapters 9 - 16.

Answer 3:
The 5th Trumpet Angel sounds at Revelation 6:1.

Answer 4:
We know the 5th Trumpet Angel is finished sounding when we are told one Woe is past.

Answer 5:
The very next thing we see happening is the 6th Trumpet Angel begins to sound. This indicates that the 5th and 6th Trumpet Angels are sounding in a sequential order. If we also look at the 6th and 7th Trumpet Angels, we will see the exact same sequential order. Absolutely nothing happens between when one angel finishes sounding and the next angel begins to sound. The first 4 Trumpet Angels and the first 6 seals are all sequential as well.

Answer 6:
We know the 7th Trumpet Angel is finished sounding when we see the words "It is done" in Revelation 16:17.

Answer 7:
The 5th, 6th and 7th Trumpet Angels span 7 years and 5 months.

Answer 8:
We see a picture of the rapture of the church taking place in Revelation 6:12-17. We then see the church assembled before the throne of God in Revelation 7:9-17.

Answer 9:
The first indicator that we probably won't instantaneously go from the church age into the tribulation period is the fact that we have located 7 years and 5 months of time accounted for in the 5th, 6th and 7th Trumpet Angels judgments. According to Daniel, the tribulation period is a time frame of 7 years and we can see that the Book of Revelation covers more than 7 years, not counting the millennial reign.

Work Sheet Answers

Worksheet Answers for Chapter 3

Answer 1:
President Nasser of Egypt, "*The national aim: the eradication of Israel.*"
President Nasser of Egypt, "*We will not accept any ... coexistence with Israel.*"
Syrian Defense Minister Hafez Assad, "*the time has come to enter into a battle of annihilation.*"
President of Iraq, Abdel Rahman Aref, "*Our goal is clear – to wipe Israel off the map.*"
President Ahmadinejad of Iran, "*The Zionist regime will be wiped out soon.*"
President Ahmadinejad of Iran, "*this regime is on its way to annihilation.*"
President Ahmadinejad of Iran, "*do its best for the annihilation of the Zionist regime.*"
Mohsen Rezaee adviser to Iran's Khamenei, "*We would raze Tel Aviv to the ground for sure.*"

Answer 2:
The Egyptian government struggled with the Muslim Brotherhood for over 60 years before the brotherhood finally gained the power of the presidency.

Answer 3:
Hosni Mubarak was the president of Egypt until Mohamed Morsi of the Muslim Brotherhood was elected president in 2011. Morsi was ousted from office by the Egyptian military in 2013.

Answer 4:
The Grand Renaissance Dam being built in Ethiopia on the Blue Nile has the potential of causing the Nile river in Egypt to dry up according to the scripture in Isaiah 19:5-6.

The Three Woes
A Guide To Understanding Revelation and End Time Prophecies

Answer 5:

Prophecy	Description	Status
Initial	Israel a nation again	Fulfilled
1st	Thine enemies make a tumult	Fulfilled
2nd	Egyptian against Egyptian	Fulfilled
3rd	Egyptians given over to a cruel lord	Fulfilled
4th	The Nile river shall dry up	potential for fulfillment
5th	Psalm 83 War	Unfulfilled
6th	Damascus a ruinous heap	Unfulfilled
7th	Desolation of Moab and Ammon	Unfulfilled
8th & 9th	Five cities of Egypt speak Hebrew	Unfulfilled
	Highway from Egypt to Assyria	Unfulfilled

Work Sheet Answers

Worksheet Answers for Chapter 4

Answer 1:

Ezekiel 38:1 - 39:8 contains three specific prophecies. The three prophecies are:

1. The War
2. The Burial of the Dead
3. The Cleanup and Burning of the Weapons of War

Answer 2:

The two prevalent descriptions for Israel at the time of Ezekiel's War are:

1. All of the Israeli people are in Israel
2. Israel is llving safely in unwalled villages

Answer 3:

The Biblical references to Gog and Magog are only found in Ezekiel Chapters 38 and 39 and in Revelation Chapter 20.

Answer 4:

Ezekiel had visions from the Lord on eleven separate occasions and they were:

	Scripture Reference	Reference Date
1.	Ezekiel 8:1	Year 6, Month 6, Day 5
2.	Ezekiel. 20:1	Year 7, Month 5, Day 10
3.	Ezekiel 24:1	Year 9, Month 10, Day 10
4.	Ezekiel 29:1	Year 10, Month 10, Day 12
5.	Ezekiel 26:1	Year 11, Day 1
6.	Ezekiel 31:1	Year 11, Month 3, Day 1
7.	Ezekiel 32:1	Year 12, Month 12, Day 1

8.	Ezekiel 32:17	Year 12 Month 12, Day 15
9.	Ezekiel 33:21	Year 12, Month 10, Day 5
10.	Ezekiel 1:1	Year 13, Month 4, Day 5
11.	Ezekiel 40:1	Year 25, Month 1, Day 10

Answer 5:

Ezekiel vision found at Ezekiel 33:21 has seven sub-visions and they are:

	Sub-Vision	Sub-Vision Description
1.	Ezekiel 33:21	The enemy inhabitants of Israel
2.	Ezekiel 34:1	Woe to the shepherds of Israel and the restoration of Israel to the land
3.	Ezekiel 35:1	Set thy face against mount Seir
4.	Ezekiel 36:1	Prophesy to the mountains of Israel
5.	Ezekiel 36:16	Prophesy to the house of Israel
6.	Ezekiel 37:1	Prophesy to the dry bones
7.	Ezekiel 37:15	The unity of Israel (Judah and Israel one)
8.	Ezekiel 38:1	Prophesy to Gog and Magog

Answer 6:

The three sub-visions of Ezekiel 33:21 that are yet to be fulfilled are:

1.	The return of the rest of Israel to the promised land
2.	The uniting of Judah with the rest of Israel under the reign of Christ
3.	The Battle of Gog and Magog

Answer 7:

The great hailstones of Revelation 16:21 will weigh as much as 75 pounds.

Work Sheet Answers

Answer 8:
A 35 pound block of ice is 29" x 14" x 5 1/2" and is about the size of four shoeboxes.

The Three Woes
A Guide To Understanding Revelation and End Time Prophecies

Worksheet Answers for Chapter 5

Answer 1:

	THE COMPONENTS OF THE OLIVET DISCOURSE	
1.	Matt. 24: 4-14	A description of the worsening conditions in the world leading up to the rapture of the church.
2.	Matt. 24:15-22	A description of a major even that will usher in the second half of the tribulation and the end of the world (the Wrath of God) as we know it.
3.	Matt. 24:23-31	A description of the rapture of the church and a description of the signs to look for just before its occurrence.
4.	Matt. 24:32 - Matt. 25:30	A description via parables of the time just prior to the rapture of the church and how the church should watch and live to be prepared for Christ's coming.
5.	Matt. 25:31-46	A picture of the Millennial Age and the end time judgments.

Answer 2:
The most significant and often repeated sign in the Olivet Discourse that Jesus tells us to watch for is Deception.

Answer 3:
Genesis 8:23 says: *"While the earth remaineth, seedtime and harvest, cold and heat, and summer and winter, and day and night shall not cease."* In this verse, God is promising us that as long as the earth remains, we will continue to have seasons and fluxions in our weather patterns but the earth will continue to sustain us.

Answer 4:
The four things, besides deception, that Jesus told us in the Olivet Discourse to watch for were:

1.	"rumors of wars and wars"
2.	"pestilences"
3.	"earthquakes"
4.	"afflictions and betrayals"

Answer 5:
People in America are being betrayed through deceit. American institutions that could once be trusted to entertain and shape the minds of American youth in a moral and positive manner, are now bastions for indoctrinating those same youth with the most extreme anti-God and anti-moral values.

The Three Woes
A Guide To Understanding Revelation and End Time Prophecies

Worksheet Answers for Chapter 6

Answer 1:
The dual threaded message to the seven churches in Asia Minor is that one thread leads to Heaven with Eternal Promises and the other thread leads to Hell with Eternal Punishment.

Answer 2:
In the Olivet Discourse of Matthew 24, Jesus said we should be watching for five things: deception, wars, famines, pestilences and persecution.

	Event	Revelation Seal	Revelation Horse
1	Deception	First Seal	White Horse
2	Wars	Second Seal	Red Horse
3	Famines	Third Seal	Black Horse
4	Pestilences	Fourth Seal	Pale Horse
5	Persecution	Fifth Seal	

Answer 3:
Revelation 6:6 is talking about famine when it says "*a measure of wheat for a penny, and three measures of barley for a penny.*" At the time when this scripture was written, a penny was equal to one days' wages. So what we are being told is that it will take one day's wages to buy one measure of wheat, or one loaf of bread. A day's wage would purchase three measures of barley, the common mans food.

Answer 4:
No, the consequences and impact that occurs due to the opening of any particular seal does not cease when the next seal is opened. The results and impacts of the seals are cumulative.

Work Sheet Answers

Answer 5:
Open Doors USA, a non-denominational mission supporting persecuted Christians around the world, estimates that persecution is now affecting 260 million Christians around the world. According to the BBC News Online, Christian persecution is "at near genocide levels."

Answer 6:
The Cosmic Signs is a term assigned to the three events that are commonly found together in the scriptures. They are:

1.	The sun being darkened
2.	The moon turning to blood
3.	The stars of heaven falling

Answer 7:
Power is given to the *scorpion* locusts to torment mankind for 5 months.

Answer 8:
In Revelation 9:12, we are told that "One woe is past;."

Answer 9:
The 6th trumpet angel begins to sound in Revelation 9:13, which begins the 2nd woe.

Answer 10:
The timeframe of the 6th trumpet angel, the 2nd woe, corresponds to the 1st half of the tribulation period.

Answer 11:
The time "*an hour, and a day, and a month and a year*" in Revelation 9:15 is indicative of a specific point in time, such as July 4, 1776, the date of Americas Declaration of Independence. It

does not refer to a span of time.

Answer 12:
The main focus of what is taking place during the 42 month time span of this 2nd woe is the ministry of the two witnesses.

Answer 13:
The exact middle of the seven year tribulation period is marked by the resurrection of the two witnesses and God's calling them "to come up hither." We are told that within one hour of this there is a great earthquake that kills 7,000 and then the 2nd woe is past.

Answer 14:
The personages that make up the Satanic Trinity in the 3rd woe are:

1.	the dragon, who is Satan
2.	the first beast, who is the antichrist
3.	a second beast, who is the false prophet

Answer 15:
Once the antichrist rises to power, he will retain his power for 42 months, which is the full duration of the time span of the 3rd woe.

Answer 16:
The mark that Christians commonly refer to as the 'mark of the beast', is really one of three distinct marks, which are:

1.	the mark of the beast
2.	the name of the beast
3.	the number of the name of the beast

Once an individual has bowed and worshipped the first beast, the antichrist, then that individual will be allowed to receive one of the three marks to indicate their submission to the beast. This worship of the first beast and submission to the antichrist guarantees a man's spiritual second death.

Answer 17:
RFID stands for Radio Frequency Identification.

Answer 18:
At the end of the 42 month time span of the 3rd woe, Christ will return with His raptured church and do battle with the army of the antichrist at a place called Armageddon. Christ and His saints will be victorious and the following will happen:

1.	the beast, the antichrist, will be taken and cast into the lake of fire
2.	the false prophet will be taken and cast into the lake of fire
3.	the Devil, Satan, will be bound for 1,000 years and cast into the bottomless pit

Answer 19:
Provide a discussion time on who the class thinks the antichrist is.

Answer 20:
In the prophecy of St. Malachy, he claims to have received a short description of each pope that would be over the Catholic church. His vision resulted in a list of 112 popes in succession, with the 112 pope being the final pope. That means that if the prophecy is true, then Pope Benedict XVI would be the last pope before the final 112th pope. In 2013 Pope Benedict XVI resigned and Pope Francis became the 112th pope. Will Pope Francis turnout to be the false prophet of Revelation Chapter 13? We don't know, but his coziness with the Muslim religion and his desire to be inclusive to all people are causing many to watch closely.

The Three Woes
A Guide To Understanding Revelation and End Time Prophecies

Note: The election of Pope Leo XIV as the 113th pope should cause the prophecy of St. Malachy to be considered debunk.

Answer 21:
Provide a discussion time on who the class thinks the false prophet could be. Do they think he is alive?

Work Sheet Answers

Worksheet Answers for Chapter 7

Answer 1:
The Jewish calendar is based on the lunar cycle which is 29.53 days long.

Answer 2:
The 1st month in the Jewish calendar is called Tishrei. The Jewish people call the 1st day of this month Rosh Hashanah. Rosh Hashanah is like our New Years day.

Answer 3:
As we were looking at the Jewish calendar system we saw that the first month of the Jewish calendar is Tishrei and it occurs during our fall months of September or October. So how can Passover that coincides with the Christian observance of Good Friday, the day of Christ's crucifixion, be defined as the first month? Passover is celebrated on the 14th day of Nissan at the time of the full moon and Nissan is the seventh month in the Jewish calendar. It is believed that it is called the first month here because Nissan was the first month following the Jewish exodus from Egypt. God wasn't referring to the first month in the calendar but the first month following the Exodus.

Answer 4:
The first four spring feast days that God ordained in Leviticus Chapter 23 are:

Jewish Feast Day	Leviticus Equivalent	Christian New Testament Equivalent
Passover	Feast of Passover	Christ's Death
Seder	Feast of Unleavened Bread	Christ's Burial
Yom HaBikkurim	Feast of First Fruits	Christ's Resurrection

| Shavuot | Festival of Weeks | Pentecost, Giving of the Holy Spirit |

Answer 5:
All four of the spring feast days have been fulfilled.

Answer 6:
The next three feast days from Leviticus 23 that have not yet been fulfilled are:

1.	The Feast of Trumpets where Christ will return in the air, to rapture His church
2.	The Feast of Atonement where Christ will return to earth and to the Battle of Armageddon at the end of the great tribulation
3.	The Feast of Tabernacles where Christ establishes His 1,000 year Millennial reign

Answer 7:
The Jewish celebration themes for Rosh Hashanah, the feast of trumpets are:

1.	Repentance
2.	Preparation for the day of Divine judgment
3.	Prayer for a fruitful year

Answer 8:
Provide a time to discuss the scripture in Matthew that says "ye know neither the day nor the hour."

Work Sheet Answers

Worksheet Answers for Chapter 8

Answer 1:
Adam and Eve were forbidden to eat from the tree of the knowledge of good and evil. God told them that they would die if they did so.

Answer 2:
God placed many trees in the Garden of Eden, but the only other tree that God named was the tree of life. The names of both of these trees were self descriptive. The one offered life and the other offered knowledge and death. Adam and Eve chose to eat from the 'tree of knowledge of good and evil'. Is seems that Adam and Eve never ate from the tree of life. Do you have any thoughts as to why?

Answer 3:
When Adam and Eve sinned, they lost their innocence and fell out of grace with God. This new human trait of being a sinful being was passed on to all their offspring causing all future humans to be born with this sinful human nature. This new sinful nature was soon displayed in the relationship between Cain and Abel.

Answer 4:
Jesus Christ was unique qualified to save us from our sins and to cleanse us from our sin nature because He Himself was a man who was not only sinless but also without the sin nature of all the rest of mankind. He was all this because His Father was God. Christ received His sinless nature from His Father God and He was qualified to redeem mankind because He got His humanity from His mother Mary.

Answer 5:
The three types of death that a man can suffer are:

1.	Physical death
2.	Spiritual death
3.	Eternal death

Answer 6:

The three components of a human being are :

1.	Spirit
2.	Body
3.	Soul

The spirit is mans essence, the body is an empty container to hold the essence and the soul is merging of the spirit and body. The soul is the living being that we all see and know as a particular individual. It is a crude example, but think of the body as an empty balloon that is shaped like a man. Fill the balloon with air and it takes shape as a man, but when the air is released, the balloon will fall to the ground and no longer retain the appearance of a man.

Answer 7:

I Corinthians 15:44 says that there is both a natural body and a spiritual body. The natural body is the human body that be each have is this life. The spiritual body is the body that all believers in Christ are promised if they confess their sins to Jesus Christ and turn from their sinful ways. This spiritual body, is called a glorified body, we are told in I Peter 1:4-5 that it is an incorruptible body, an undefiled body, and that it will not fade not away, or in other words, it will not age and cease to exist like a human body. This spiritual body will only be given to those who live for Jesus Christ.

Answer 8:
The spirit of all those who do not receive a glorified body will have their part in the lake which burneth with fire and brimstone.

The Three Woes
A Guide To Understanding Revelation and End Time Prophecies

Worksheet Answers for Chapter 9

Answer 1:
According to God, mans purpose in life is to fellowship with God. God made man because He desired a being who would chose to love Him and live for Him of his own free will.

Answer 2:
If an individual misses the rapture of the church and ends into the tribulation period, the only way for that individual to escape the lake of fire is to be beheaded instead of bowing to worship the beast and taking the mark of the beast.

Answer 3:
During the 1,000 year Millennial Reign of Christ, the saints of God will be assigned the task of judging, executing judgment and executing vengeance.

Answer 4:
Provide a time to discuss the 45 days that Daniel talks about in Daniel 12:10-12.

Answer 5:
At the end of the Battle of Armageddon the following will take place:

1.	The beast, who is also called the Antichrist, is cast alive into the lake of fire for all of eternity
2.	The false prophet is cast alive into the lake of fire for all of eternity
3.	The dragon who is the devil and Satan is bound a thousand years and cast into the bottomless pit

Work Sheet Answers

Answer 6:
At the end of the 1,000 year Millennial Reign of Christ, the dragon who is the devil and Satan will be released to once again deceive the nations for a period of time. He will engage Gog and Magog to do battle with the saints of God. This Battle of Gog and Magog seems like it is probably what most people today call Ezekiel's war.

Answer 7:
At the end of the Millennial Reign, Satan is released and he and his followers encompass the saints. Then God sends fire down from heaven and devours them. Satan is then cast into the lake of fire forever and ever, where the antichrist and the false prophet have been for the past thousand years.

Answer 8:
New Jerusalem is the city of God that most people are describing when they are describing what heaven will be like.

Answer 9:
The city new Jerusalem is a perfect cube.

Answer 10:
Each side of the city new Jerusalem is approximately 1,377 miles. It is also 1,377 miles high. This is just a few miles less than the 1,386 miles that Detroit, Michigan is from Miami, Florida.

Answer11:
The only residents of the new Jerusalem will those who have their name written it the Book of Life. The new Jerusalem is God's replacement for the Garden of Eden. The tree of life is there, the water of life is there, God is there and man is there. This time though, only individuals who have had their sins washed away and covered by the blood of the Lamb, Jesus Christ, will be there.

Worksheet Answers for Chapter 10

Answer 1:
God's most prized possession is mankind. He was willing for His only son to die a gruesome death on the cross to redeem us and to atone for our sins.

Answer 2:
According to the law of the kinsman redeemer, the new owner of the land could not keep the land if the original owner had the means to pay the price to redeem the land. In Peter, we are told that Christ died; shedding His sinless blood to redeem us from the debt of sin we are all bound to. We only need to avail ourselves to His redemption.

Answer 3:
The law of the kinsman redeemer specified that the redeemer had to be a qualified relative. This is why John wept when initially no man was found to open the book. He knew an angel wouldn't do, the redeemer had to be a man.

Answer 4:
When Christ was born of the virgin Mary, He met the condition of being a kinsman redeemer because He became a part of the human race. When Christ died a sinless death on the cross, He earned the right to redeem the earth back from Satan. Jesus earned not only the right to redeem the earth but to also redeem God's lost possession, mankind. The shedding of His innocent and worthy blood legally discharged the lien on the souls of all men.

Answer 5:
Christ earned the right to redeem the earth and mankind over two thousand years ago, but He has not yet claimed that right. As

Work Sheet Answers

we have said and proved throughout this book, the seals are in the process of being opened, but that opening process is not yet complete. When we see the words "It is done" in Revelation 16:17, the angel is telling us that the last seal has been opened and that the redemption, reclaiming and cleansing of the earth is complete.

Answer 6:
The four beasts and the four and twenty elders in Revelation Chapter 5 are Christ's witnesses that He is qualified and worthy to make the payment to reclaim that which had been lost by Adam.

Answer 7:
We are told in Ephesians 1:13-14 that the Holy Spirit is the down payment of our redemptive purchase by Christ until the last seal has been opened and the title deed claimed.

Answer 8:
The four titles given to Jesus in the Gospels are:

1.	As the Son of David, He has the right to claim title to the Throne of David
2.	As the Son of Abraham, He has the right to claim title to the Land of Israel, as defined in Genesis
3.	As the Son of Man, He has the right to claim title to the Earth
4.	As the Son of God, He is the Heir of All Things

Worksheet Answers for Chapter 11

Answer 1:
The purpose for the separation of church and state in our society was to keep the influence of the state out of the church. The anti-faith, anti-god based segment of our society has worked diligently to twist the meaning and intent of the founding fathers. Today, it is more about keeping the church from having any influence over the state than keeping the state out of the church.

Answer 2:
Provide a time to discuss how America's school system has changed from a spiritual based system to a secular based system.

Answer 3:
In 1954 Senator Lyndon B. Johnson introduced a bill that made it illegal for a church to openly speak out against anything that the government declared "legal," even if it is immoral, such as abortion or homosexuality, etc.

Answer 4:
On Sunday. These laws were not based on concerns that workers deserved a day of rest. Instead, they were meant to respect the Christian Sabbath and were directed at personal activities regarded as moral offenses, such as gambling or the consumption of alcohol.

Answer 5:
Provide a time to discuss how America is honoring God's Sabbath.

Work Sheet Answers

Answer 6:

Following the destruction of Israel and the Babylonian captivity, the people sought God through the following acts:

1.	By fasting and confessing the sins and iniquities of their fathers
2.	They read the Word one fourth part of the day
3.	They made a covenant to keep the law as given by Moses

NOTES

Work Sheet Answers

NOTES

NOTES

Biblical Lineage Charts

The Three Woes
A Guide To Understanding Revelation and End Time Prophecies

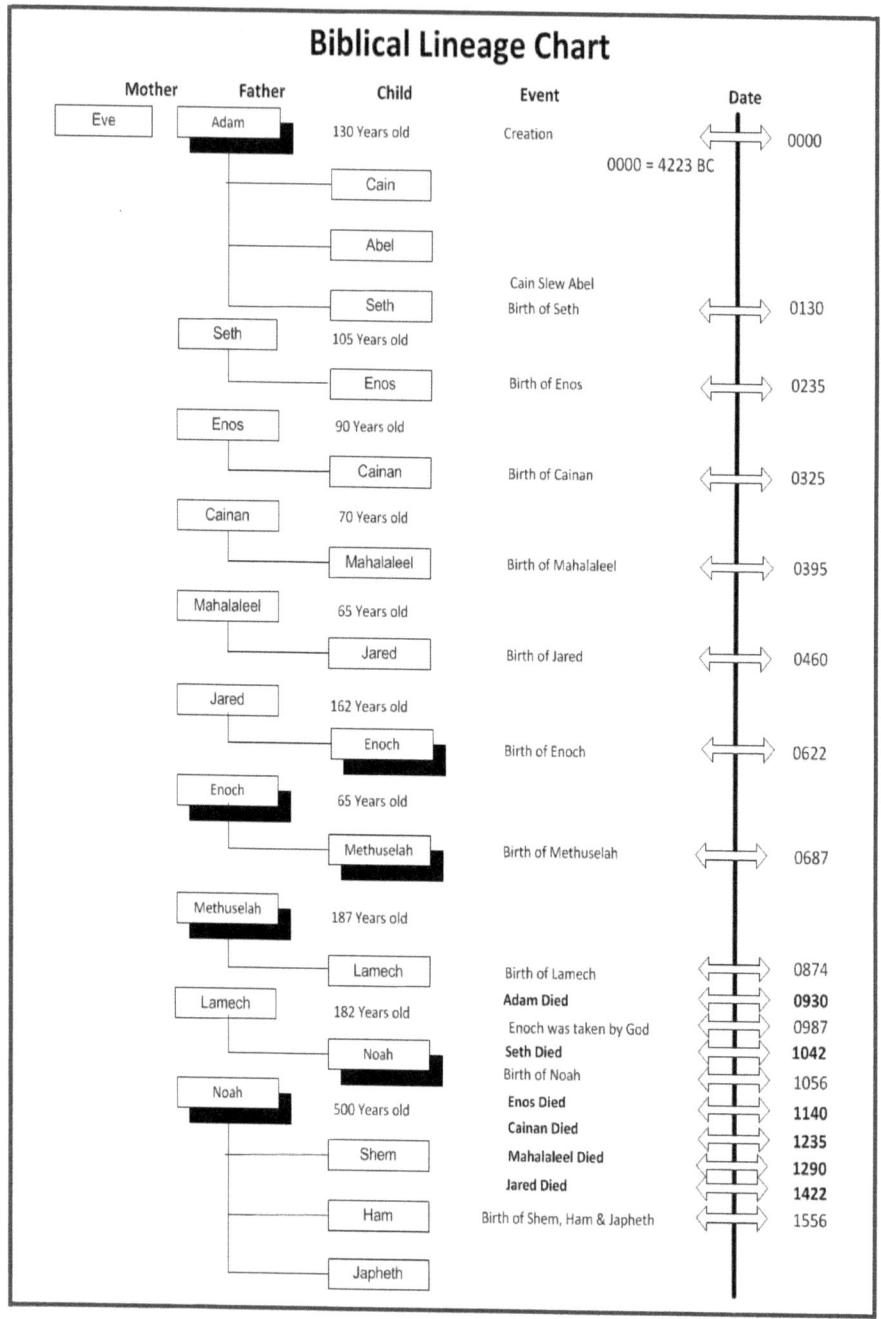

Biblical Lineage Charts

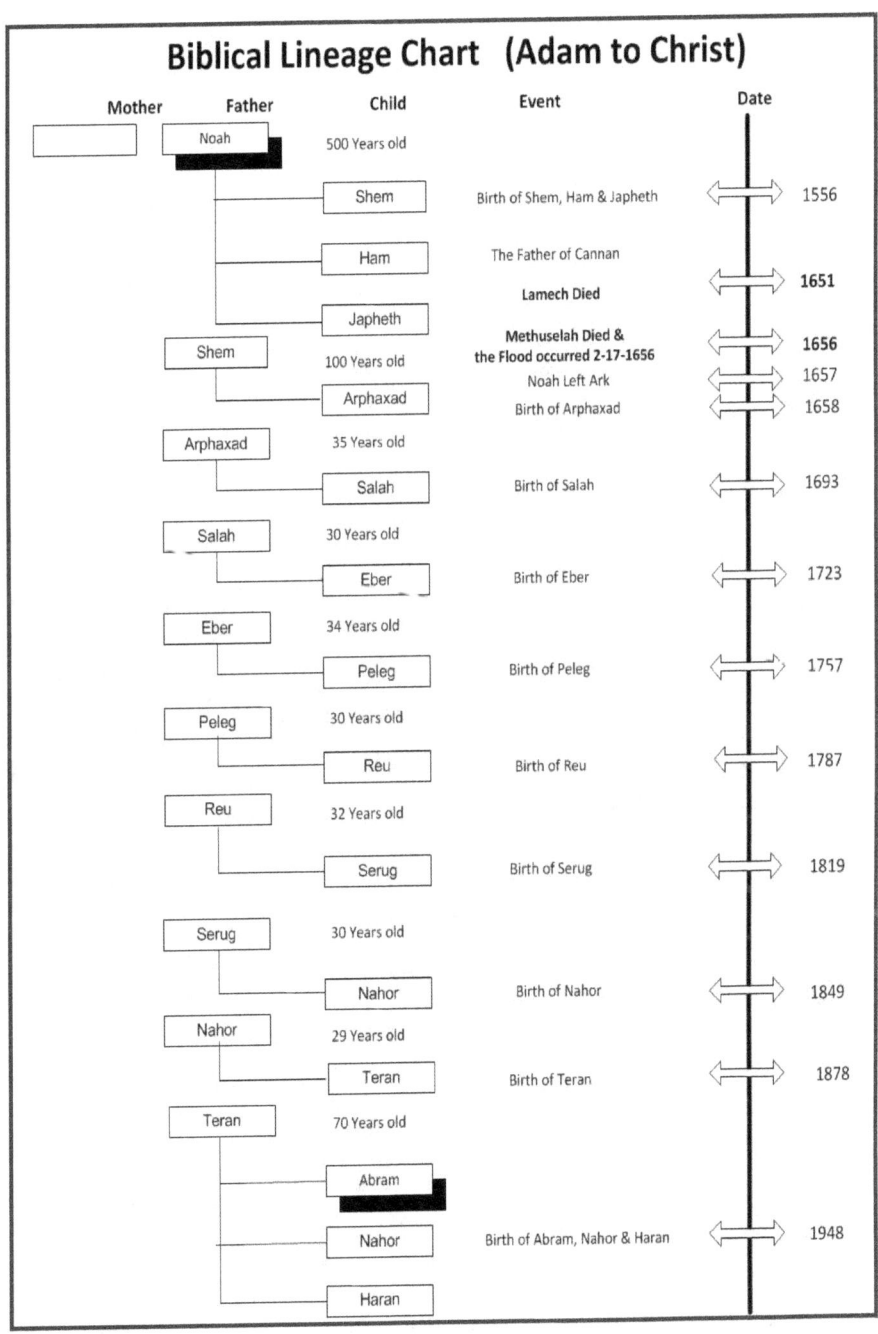

The Three Woes
A Guide To Understanding Revelation and End Time Prophecies

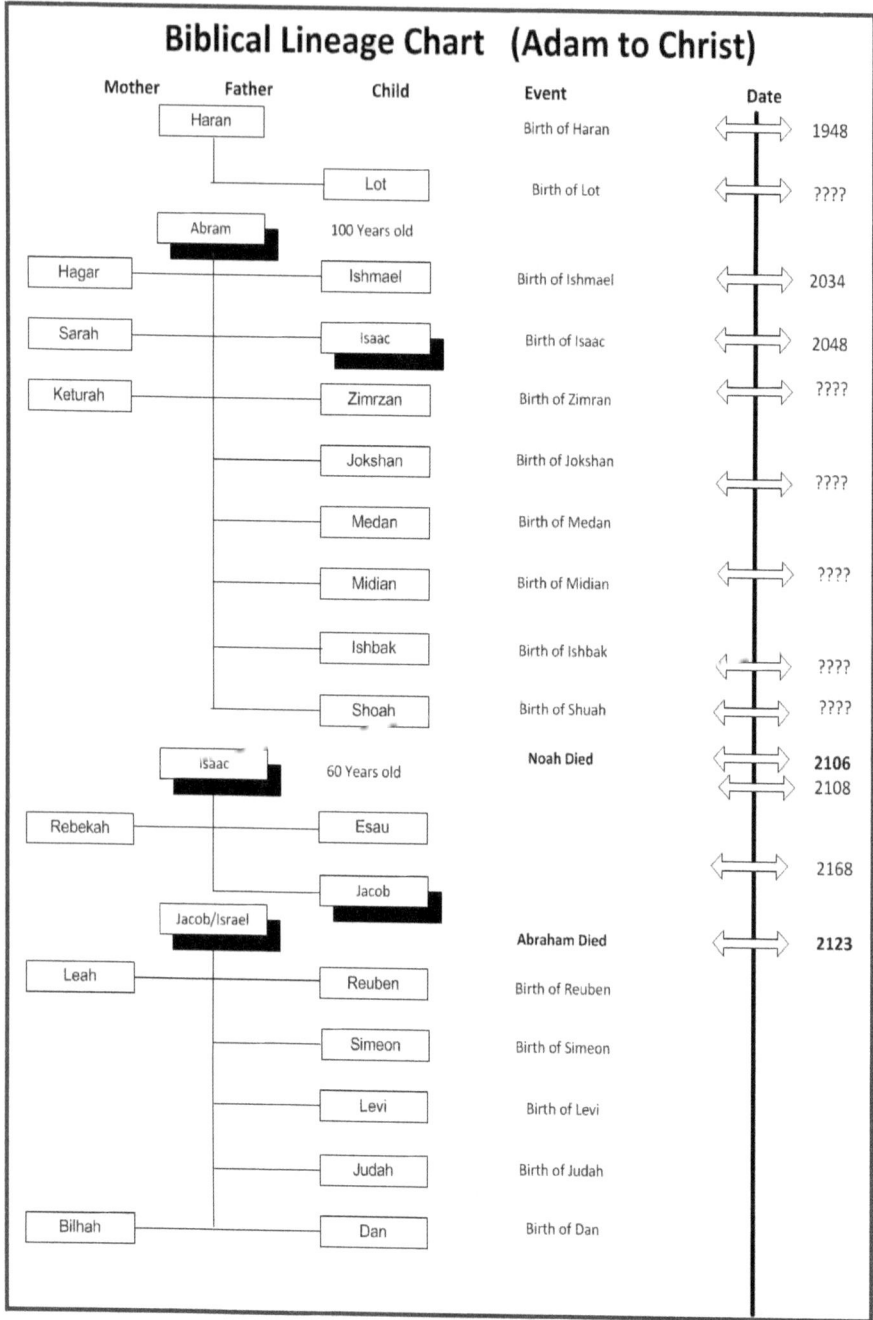

Biblical Lineage Charts

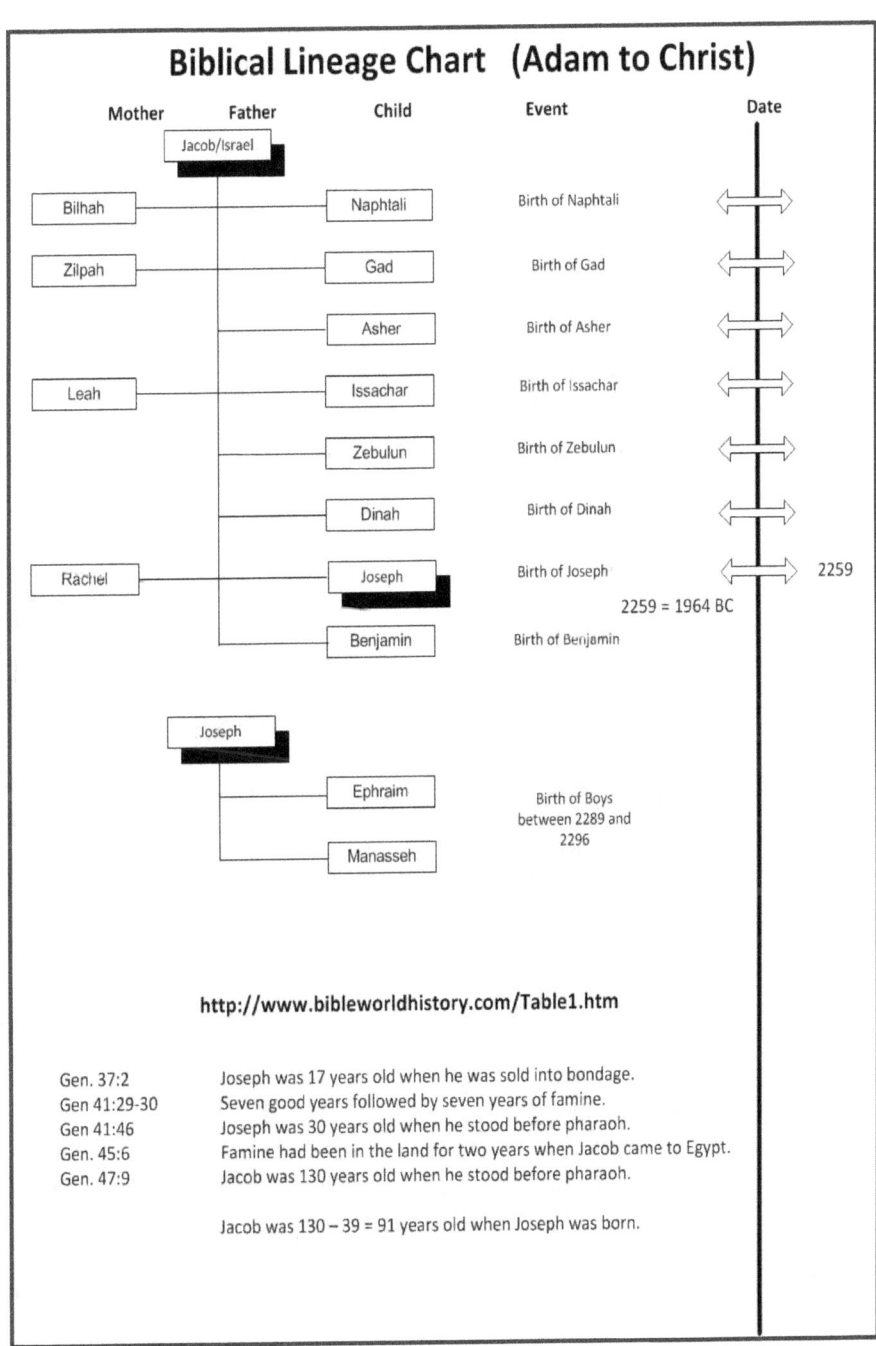

Bible Lineage Chronology

0000	Adam Created
0130	Seth Born
0235	Enos Born
0325	Cainan Born
0395	Mahalaleel Born
0460	Jared Born
0622	Enoch Born
0687	Methuselah Born
0874	Lamech Born
0930	Adam Died
0987	Enoch was taken by God
1042	Seth Died
1056	Noah Born
1140	Enos Died
1235	Cainan Died
1290	Mahalaleel Died
1422	Jared Died
1556	Shem, Ham, Japheth Born (Triplets ?)
1651	Lamech Died
1656	Methuselah Died
1656	The Flood
1657	Noah left the Ark
1658	Arphaxad Born
1693	Salah Born
1723	Eber Born
1757	Peleg Born
1787	Reu Born
1819	Serug Born
1849	Nahor Born
1878	Teran Born

Biblical Lineage Charts

1948	Abram, Nahor, Haran Born (Triplets ?)	
	(Abram became Abraham)	
1958	Sara Born	(Became Sarah)
????	Lot Born to Haran	
1996	Peleg Died	
1997	Nahor Died	
2006	Noah Died	
????	Haran Died	
2026	Reu Died	
2034	Ishmael Born	
2048	Isaac Born	
2049	Serug Died	
2083	Teran Died	
2085	Sarah Died	(Was called Sara)
2088	Isaac Married Rebekah	
2096	Arphaxad Died	
2108	Esau, Jacob Born Twins	(Jacob became Israel)
2123	Abraham Died	(Abraham was Abram)
2126	Salah Died	
2158	Shem Died	
2171	Ishmael Died	
2187	Eber Died	

The Twelve (12) Tribes of Israel (Jacob)   (The Jewish People)

21__	Reuben Born	21__	Dan Born
21__	Simeon Born	21__	Naphtali Born
21__	Levi Born	21__	Gad Born
21__	Judah Born	21__	Asher Born
21__	Issachar Born	2198	Joseph Born
21__	Zebulun Born	22__	Benjamin Born

2215	Joseph sold into Egypt at age of 17
2228	Isaac Died

The Three Woes
A Guide To Understanding Revelation and End Time Prophecies

2237	Joseph spent 2 years in Egypt's prison Gen. 41:1 Joseph stood before Pharaoh at age of 30 Gen. 41:46 + 7 good years + 2 bad years Gen 45:6 – Joseph spoke to brethren, father not arrived yet)
2238	Jacob took his people to Egypt Gen 47:9 Land of Rameses mentioned in Gen 47:11
2255	Jacob Died (Jacob was Israel)
2308	Joseph Died

The Twelve sons of Ishmael

Nebajoth	Massa
Kedar	Hadar
Adbeel	Tema
Mibsam	Jetur
Mishma	Naphish
Dumah	Kedemah

Israel   (The Nation) spent 430 years in Egypt

Levi lived 137 years,   Kohath 133 years,
Amram 137 years, then Aaron & Moses were born

2585	Aaron Born
2588	Moses Born
2628	Joshua Born
2668	The Exodus
2708	Moses Died
2738	Joshua Died

Study Material Resources

For Quantity Discount Pricing

Go To

WWW.3WOES.COM

"The Three Woes"   20 copies $229
"A Guide to Understanding Revelation and End Time Prophecies"

Each additional copy $11.45 each

That's a savings of $79

OR

"The Three Woes"   20 copies $299
"Making Revelation Simple"

Each additional copy $14.95 each

That's a savings of $100

Prices Subject to Change

Technisys Corp.

The Three Woes
A Guide To Understanding Revelation and End Time Prophecies

To Purchase Additional Study Resources Go To:

WWW.3WOES.COM

Understanding Revelation's

Three Woes

Revelation Time Lines Found in the Three Woes

Rev. 8:13
Woe, woe, woe to the inhibitors of the earth because of the three angels yet to sound.

Start	Rev. 9:1	And the fifth *trumpet* angel sounded
	Rev. 9:2-5	Locusts from the bottomless pit have power to torment men five months
Stop	Rev. 9:12	One woe is past

Start	Rev. 9:13	And the sixth *trumpet* angel sounded
	Rev. 9:14-15	The sixth angel loosed four angels from Euphrates river to slay a third of men for an hour, and a day, and a month and a year | *A point in time*
	Rev. 11:2-3	The holy city shall be tread under foot by the Gentiles for forty two months | *These times*
		Two witnesses given power to prophesy for | *coincide with*
		a thousand two hundred and three score days | *one another*
	Rev. 11:7	The two witnesses complete their prophesy and are killed by the beast that is described by the seventh *trumpet* angel.
Stop	Rev. 11:14	The second woe is past

Start	Rev. 11:15	The seventh *trumpet* angel sounded
	Rev. 12:1-3	A woman (Israel) appears in heaven - A great red dragon appears in heaven
	Rev. 12:6	The woman (Israel) flees to the wilderness for a thousand two hundred and three score days
	Rev. 12:12	Woe to the inhabiters of the earth
	Rev. 12:13-14	The serpent (*dragon*) persecutes the woman for a time, and times and half a time *These times will coincide*
	Rev. 13:1-7	The beast makes war with the saints for forty two months and over comes them. These saints are the Israeli people who turned to God through the ministry of the two witnesses and the 144,000 sealed children of Israel.
Stop	Rev. 16:17	It is done.

Chart 2

Color 8.5" by 11" laminated
"Understanding Revelation Three Woes" Chart 2

Study Material Resources

To Purchase Additional Study Resources Go To:

WWW.3WOES.COM

Copyright © 2023 by Barney Rapp

	Angelic Proclamation	Resulting Punishment	
Rev. 8:13 Woe, woe, woe to the inhabitants of the earth because of the three angels yet to sound.	**Fifth Angel** — Rev. 9:1 And the fifth angel sounded; Rev. 9:2-5 Locusts torment men five months; Rev. 9:12 One woe is past.	**1st Woe** — Rev. 9:2-5 Locusts from the bottomless pit have power to torment men 5 months	Five Months
	Sixth Angel — Rev. 9:13 And the sixth angel sounded; Rev. 9:14-15 Angels kill mankind; Rev. 11:2-3 Holy City taken; Rev. 11:3-12 Two witnesses; Rev. 11:14 The second woe is past	**2nd Woe** — Rev. 9:14-15 Four angels from Euphrates river to slay a third of men for an hour, and a day, and a month and a year; Rev. 11:2-3 The holy city shall be tread under foot by the gentiles for forty two months; Rev. 11:3-12 My two witnesses shall prophesy a thousand two hundred and three score days	3.5 years
	Seventh Angel — Rev. 11:15 The seventh angel sounded; Rev. 12:6 Woman flees to wilderness; Rev. 12:13-14 Serpent persecutes woman; Rev. 13:1-7 The beast makes war with the saints; Rev. 16:17 It is done. (3rd Woe past)	**3rd Woe** — Rev. 12:6 The woman flees to the wilderness for a thousand two hundred and three score days; Rev. 12:13-14 The serpent (dragon) persecutes the woman for a time, and times and half a time; Rev. 13:1-7 The beast makes war with the saints for forty two months and over comes them	3.5 years
		The Seven Years of Jacob's Trouble	

Chart 4

Color 8.5" by 11" laminated Chart 4 on "Rev.8:13" and the Three Woes

The Three Woes
A Guide To Understanding Revelation and End Time Prophecies

To Purchase Additional Study Resources Go To:

WWW.3WOES.COM

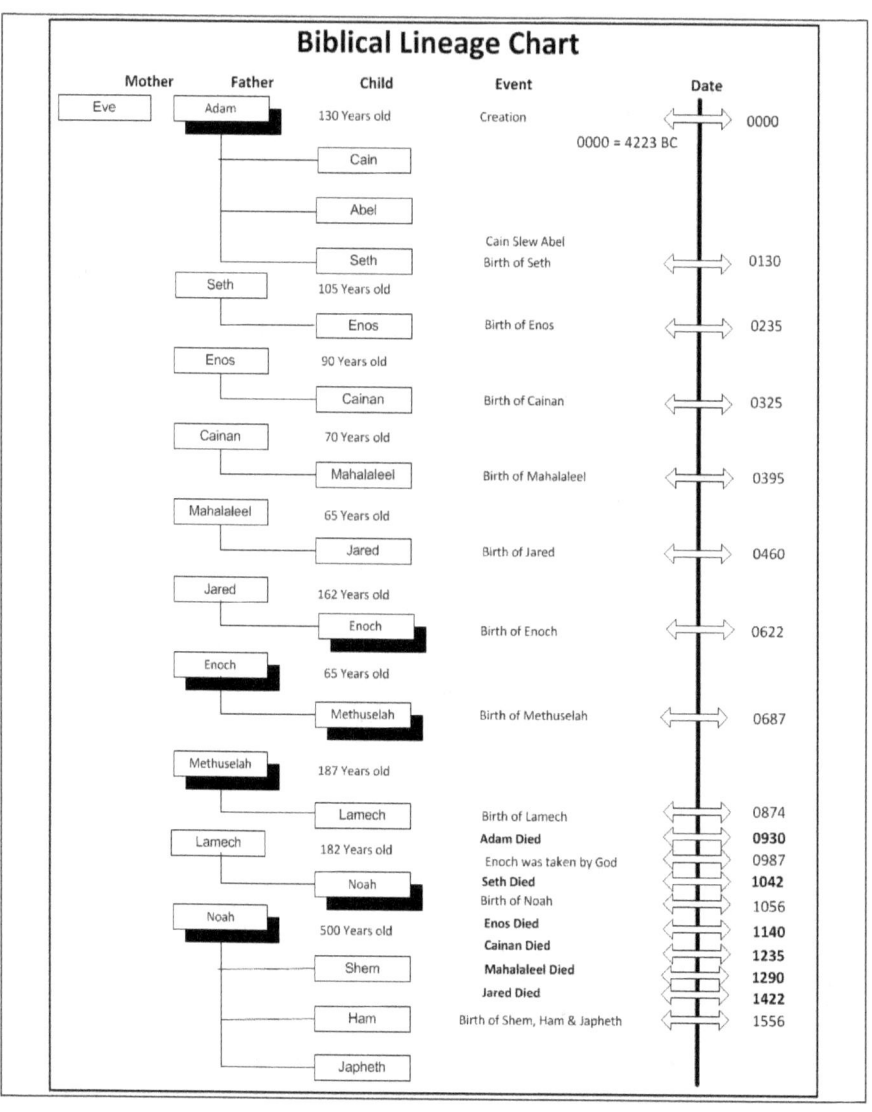

8.5" by 11" laminated "Biblical Lineage Chart" Four Page Set

Study Material Resources

To Purchase Additional Study Resources Go To:

WWW.3WOES.COM

The Jewish Feast Days Ordained by God in Leviticus

Jewish Feast Day	Ordained by God in Leviticus
Passover	In the fourteenth day of the first month at even is the Lord's passover. Leviticus 23:5 KJV
Seder	And on the fifteenth day of the same month is the feast of unleavened bread unto the Lord: seven days ye must eat unleavened bread. Leviticus 23:6 KJV
Yom HaBikkurim	Ye shall bring out of your habitations two wave loaves of two tenth deals: they shall be of fine flour; they shall be baken with leaven; they are the firstfruits unto the Lord. Leviticus 23:17 KJV
Shavuot	Even unto the morrow after the seventh sabbath shall ye number fifty days; and ye shall offer a new meat offering unto the Lord. Leviticus 23:16 KJV
Rosh Hashanah	Speak unto the children of Israel, saying, In the seventh month, in the first day of the month, shall ye have a sabbath, a memorial of blowing of trumpets, an holy convocation. Leviticus 23:24 KJV
Yom Kippur	Also on the tenth day of this seventh month there shall be a day of atonement: it shall be an holy convocation unto you; and ye shall afflict your souls, and offer an offering made by fire unto the Lord. Leviticus 23:27 KJV
Sukkot	Speak unto the children of Israel, saying, The fifteenth day of this seventh month shall be the feast of tabernacles for seven days unto the Lord. Leviticus 23:34 KJV

Jewish Feast Day	Leviticus Equivalent	Christian New Testament Equivalent	Status
Passover	Feast of Passover	Christ's Death	Fulfilled
Seder	Feast of Unleavened Bread	Christ's Burial	Fulfilled
Yom HaBikkurim	Feast of First Fruits	Christ's Resurrection	Fulfilled
Shavuot	Festival of Weeks	Pentecost, Giving of the Holy Spirit	Fulfilled
Rosh Hashanah	Feast of Trumpets	Christ's Return to Rapture His Church	unfulfilled
Yom Kippur	Feast of Atonement	Christ's Return to Earth	unfulfilled
Sukkot	Feast of Tabernacles	Christ's 1,000 Year Millennial Reign	unfulfilled

Color 8.5" by 11" laminated "Jewish Feast days Ordained by God in Leviticus" Table Text

The Three Woes
A Guide To Understanding Revelation and End Time Prophecies

To Purchase Additional Study Resources Go To:

WWW.3WOES.COM

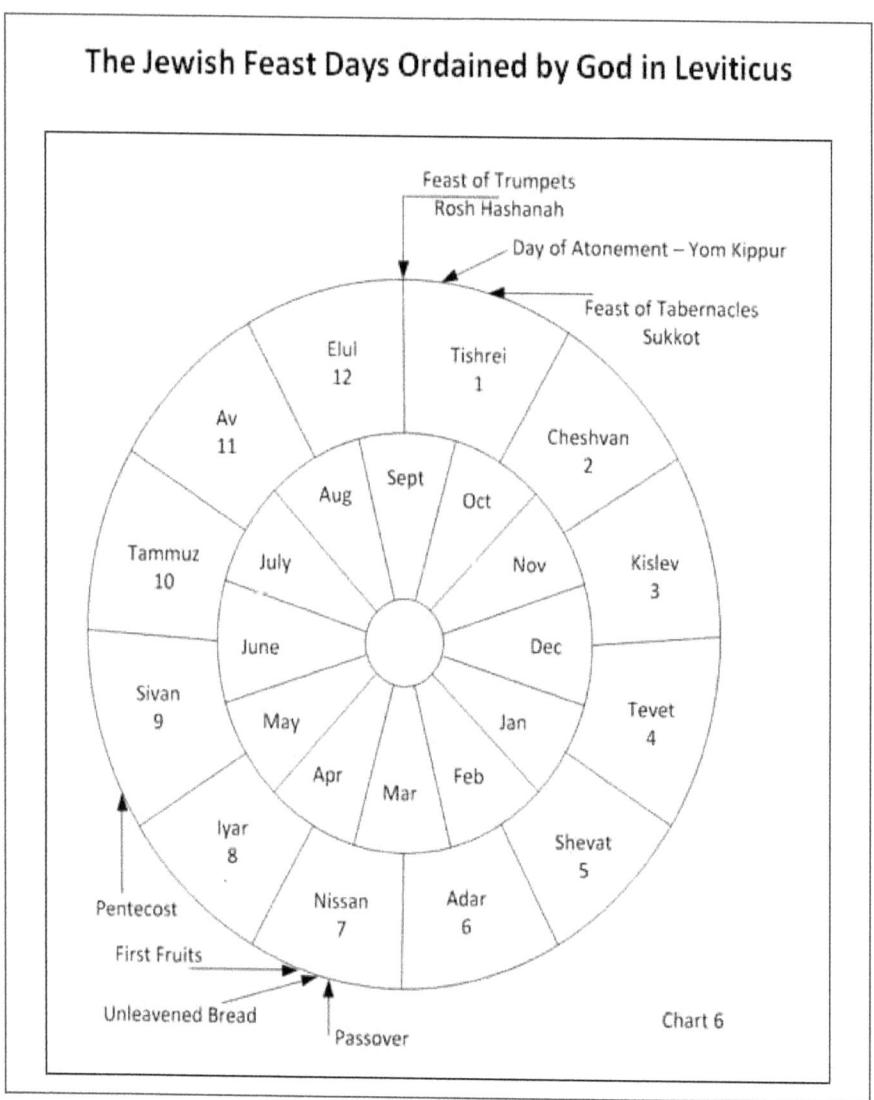

Color 8.5" by 11" laminated
"Jewish Feast days Ordained by God in Leviticus" Chart 6

Study Material Resources

To Purchase Additional Study Resources Go To:

WWW.3WOES.COM

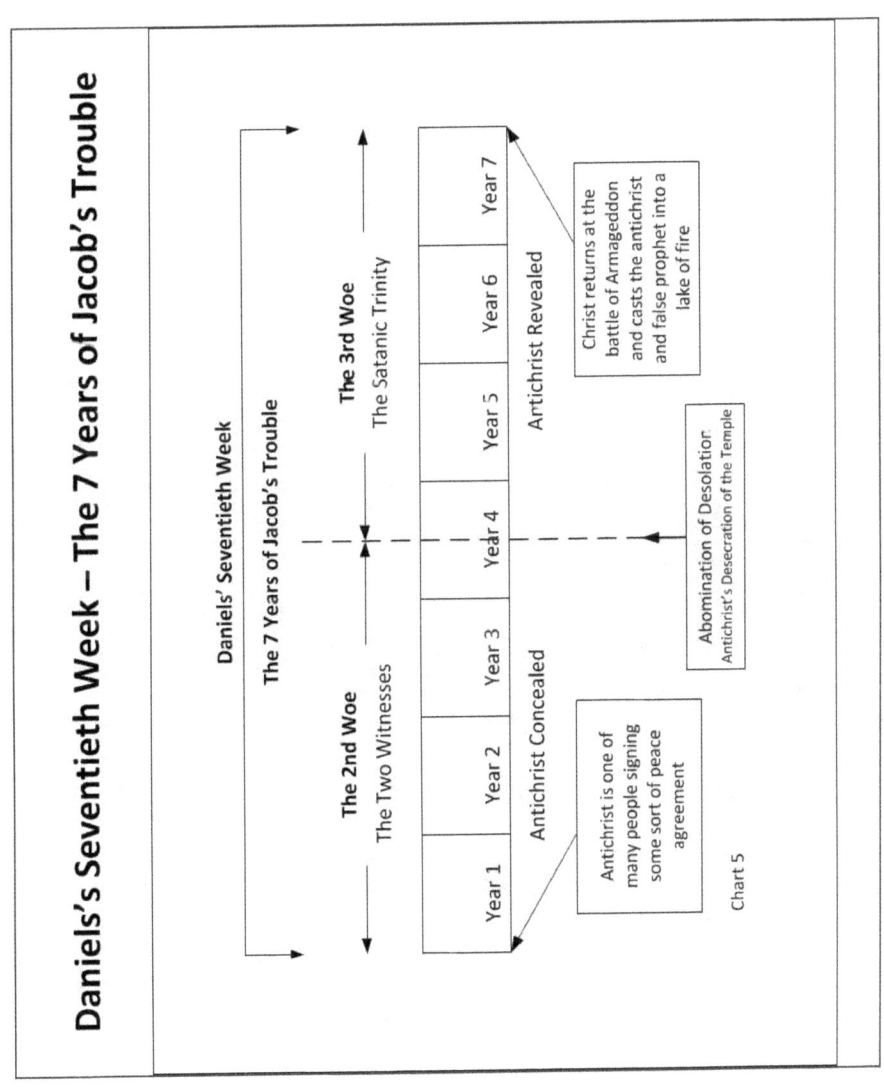

8.5" by 11" Daniel's Seventieth Week Chart 5

The Three Woes
A Guide To Understanding Revelation and End Time Prophecies

To Purchase Additional Study Resources Go To:

WWW.3WOES.COM

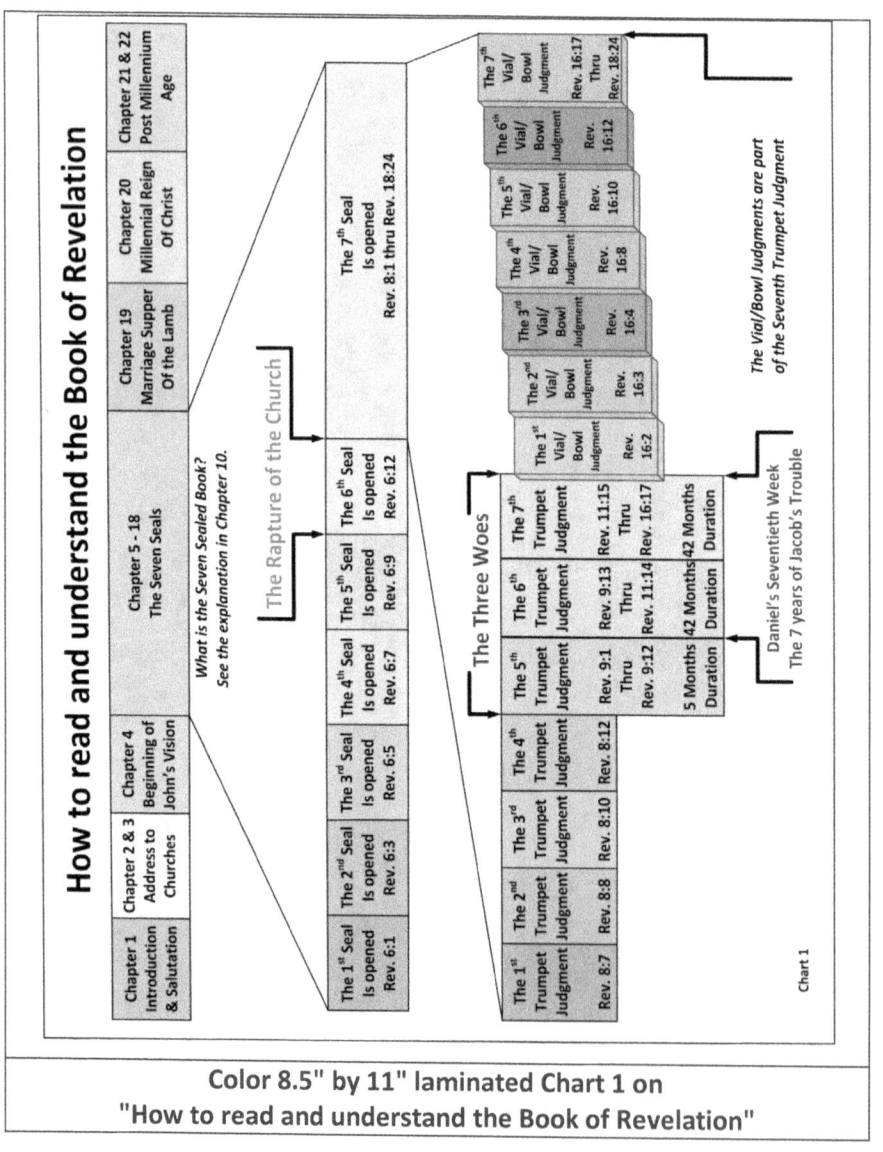

Color 8.5" by 11" laminated Chart 1 on
"How to read and understand the Book of Revelation"

Study Material Resources

Are you thinking of teaching your own class on Revelation?

A PowerPoint Slide Presentation with over 400 Slides is available free of charge.

Contact Barney Rapp at: brapp9800@gmail.com
Or visit us at:

WWW.3WOES.COM

Or find us on Facebook at:

https://www.facebook.com/3Woes-110128284042788

The Three Woes
A Guide To Understanding Revelation and End Time Prophecies

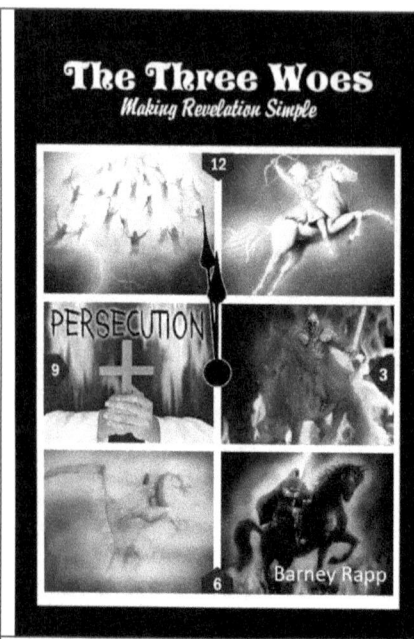

The Three Woes:
A Guide to Understanding Revelation and End Time Prophecies

The Three Woes:
 Making Revelation Simple

The Three Woes:
A Revelation Commentary

The Three Woes:
The New Jerusalem

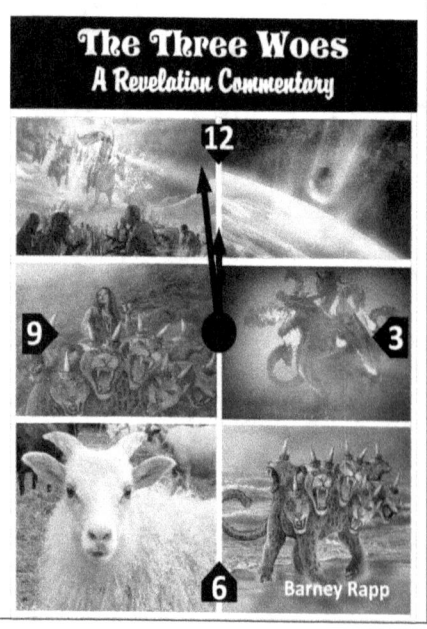

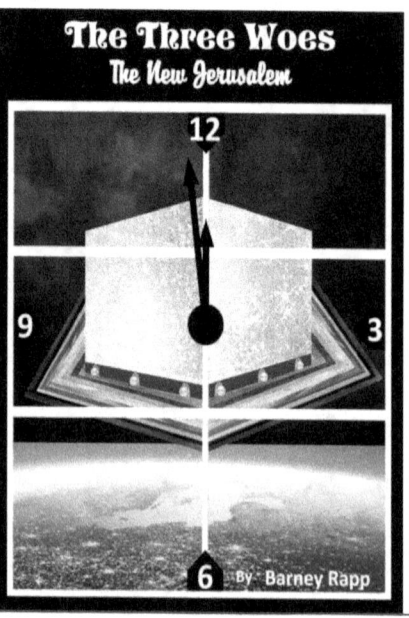

www.ingramcontent.com/pod-product-compliance
Lightning Source LLC
Chambersburg PA
CBHW052017070526
44584CB00016B/1787